TALENT WAR!

THE UNINTENDED CONSEQUENCES
OF A BROKEN HIRING PROCESS

JERMAINE WILLIAMSON

Editing, Design, and Distribution by Bublish, Inc.

Paperback ISBN: 9781647041236
eBook ISBN: 9781647041243

CONTENTS

INTRODUCTION. VII

CHAPTER 1 . . . . **1**
Your Hiring Process Is Broken, and It Is Costing You.

CHAPTER 2 . . . . **12**
Humans Are Not Widgets. There Will Be Hiring Mistakes.

CHAPTER 3 . . . . **21**
How Can You Differentiate Your Company?

CHAPTER 4 . . . . **30**
Diversity Hiring Is Simply The Right Thing to Do.

CHAPTER 5 . . . . **45**
Rip off the Bandage! Your Job Postings Need Work.

CHAPTER 6 . . . . **53**
You Don't Need to Interview 10 Candidates.

CHAPTER 7 . . . . **62**

Are Your Mission, Vision, and Values a Cultural Priority?

CHAPTER 8 . . . . **73**

Want to Hit Your Revenue Goals? Hire Faster!

CHAPTER 9 . . . . **88**

Guess What Your Candidates Are Saying?

CHAPTER 10 . . . . **100**

Your Employees Are Great! Let Them Help.

CHAPTER 11 . . . . **113**

Overcome Your Fears and Win the Talent War!

CONCLUSION. 125

INTRODUCTION

Many of my friends and professional colleagues talk to me about their frustrations around not meeting hiring, revenue, and employee growth goals. They come to me because I've been in the people business for more than 25 years. I've seen it all. My experience has shown me repeatedly that an effective hiring strategy and process is very closely tied to revenue growth. They go hand in hand. If your hiring process is humming along and allowing you to onboard top talent efficiently, chances are your revenue is humming along, too.

In writing *Talent War!* I hope to provide a resource to help others understand that often the solution to their business problems is right before their eyes: They need to fix their broken hiring process. They just have to step back and look at their hiring process without the rose-colored glasses. Most companies don't even know they have a people problem; they think they have a revenue problem or an innovation problem or some other problem. My experience has shown me that most of the time, the real problem, the underlying problem, has to do with a broken hiring process that has multiple negative impacts on the business as a whole. Top talent is central to a company's growth, productivity, morale, and innovation.

Through my many years on the front lines of talent acquisition, I have fixed almost every hiring problem imaginable. I know how to diagnose hiring issues quickly and implement solutions in record time. In virtually every industry imaginable, both domestic and international, I have helped companies and individuals address and solve their most pressing, critical, and urgent hiring challenges. This book is a compilation of what I have learned through these years of experience on the front lines of the competitive battle for talent. The pages of this book contain stories and actionable steps you can take to understand your organization's hiring challenges, tackle problems in your recruiting process, uncover missed recruitment opportunities, define your competitive advantage in the talent marketplace, and ultimately win the *Talent War!*

Since founding my company, JLW Consulting, in 2017, I've been brought in to work with many companies in the middle of hiring crises. Because top talent is so central to success, hiring problems cause a lot of stress for everyone involved: leadership teams, HR, hiring managers, recruiters, and even candidates. Typically, it's a pretty difficult situation to enter. Whether the problems are due to poor communication, human error, or not having a clear hiring process, I've watched these companies struggle mightily to diagnose big hiring issues and solve them. With every new assignment, the companies and industries change, but the goal always remains the same: unearth the real reasons why a company is struggling to hire top talent, identify solutions in a timely fashion, and turn things around. It's about strengthening each company's hiring processes and identifying and removing bottlenecks that prevent them from reaching their potential. I've watched broken hiring processes stymie growth, and efficient hiring process grows companies to exorbitant heights. My career and my company were built to address the severity and prevalence of these problems and the need to create custom hiring solutions to fix them.

I won't make false promises to you. This book can only help your company fix its hiring process with the support of management, hiring managers, leaders, recruiters, and the entire team. You can't go it alone. Everyone must come together to identify hiring problems, create solutions, and implement them. We'll cover ways to start those conversations. The solutions outlined in *Talent War!* have been proven time and time again. They work. But until they become baked into your company's DNA, you will continue to struggle to attract, hire, onboard and retain top talent. Let's turn things around and get your company back on track. I'm here to help you fix your broken hiring process. It's time for your company to reap the benefits of an effective and efficient hiring process to attract, onboard, and retain top talent in your industry.

CHAPTER 1
YOUR HIRING PROCESS IS BROKEN, AND IT IS COSTING YOU.

"You don't build a business, you build people, then people build the business."
– Zig Ziglar, motivational speaker –

I n my early days as a human resources and talent acquisition executive, I clearly remember being summoned to a meeting with my boss Kevin, the senior vice president of human resources for a large contractor that provided technical solutions to the U.S. Government. Kevin was deeply concerned about the number of open positions. Since the company's lifeblood was billable hours, these unfilled positions meant the company was losing revenue hourly. If the positions remained unfilled, he knew this could cost our company several million dollars annually.

"Jermaine," Kevin asked me, "how are you going to fix this?"

It's a common question asked of those responsible for leading hiring efforts. If your company cannot hire talent in a timely manner, it will negatively impact several areas of your organization, including revenue, growth, employee productivity, and morale. If your staff is overworked because you cannot recruit, hire, and onboard talent efficiently and effectively, it will ultimately lead to unexpected attrition and increasing paid time off (PTO) requests from your employees. Meanwhile, the work keeps mounting, and you can't deliver for you clients, shareholders, and other stakeholders. Add in the stranglehold that an inefficient hiring process puts on revenue, and it's clear that this presents a big problem for companies.

My response to Kevin was another question: "Do you know how long it takes to extend an employment offer and onboard a candidate in our organization right now?" I was asking Kevin about the metric commonly known as "time to hire." I knew for a fact that he didn't know the answer, but he took a guess anyway.

"Two weeks?" Kevin sounded more like he was asking me a question than giving me an answer.

"No," I shook my head.

"A month?" Kevin looked more alarmed as he made this second guess.

"No," I shook my head again. "Unfortunately, it is taking our company *more than two months* from the initial recruiter engagement to the day our hired candidate attends his or her new employee orientation—two months!"

Kevin's expression dropped as reality hit him. "Over two months for *each* hire?"

"Yes," I confirmed reluctantly, "over two months for each hire."

With a look of pure frustration, Kevin moaned, "We will never be able to fill our 300 plus openings at this pace! What's causing such delays?"

"It's our hiring process, Kevin. It's broken. Interview selection and hiring decisions are taking entirely too long. Something has got to change. We're losing revenue. These delays are catastrophic to the growth of our bottom line."

"Ok, let's do everything we can to fix this so we can increase hires and capture the potential revenue we're missing," Kevin said with determination.

"Great! I will need your influence to help me change the urgency and behaviors around our hiring process." I headed back to my office to begin my new assignment.

START BY RECOGNIZING THE PROBLEM

Even though Kevin had a big problem on his hands, he was one of the lucky ones. At least he had recognized that he had a problem, and he had me to help him fix it. Most companies don't even realize their hiring process is broken. Instead, executive teams focus on more visible areas within an organization as the root cause of lackluster growth, inefficiencies, and employee attrition. They look right past the hiring process and work instead on areas like marketing and sales or employee compensation and benefits. But all too often, it's a broken hiring process that's wreaking havoc within an organization.

How can you know whether the hiring process is broken at your company? Start by reviewing your company's internal hiring practices. Ask key questions of *all* the stakeholders impacted by the performance and effectiveness of your hiring process. If leadership is citing unfilled job positions and stymied growth in the same conversation, that's a sign that something's broken in your hiring process. Here's a handy list of problems that might signal that you have a broken hiring process:

- You're not attracting enough candidates
- You're not attracting the right candidates
- Your candidates are accepting jobs elsewhere
- Your hires are not a good cultural fit and have attitude problems
- Your interview process doesn't help your company differentiate between high and low-performing candidates
- Your hiring process hasn't changed, or even been evaluated in ten years
- You're discovering that you don't need to fill the position you thought you needed to fill or your team is arguing about it.

- Interviews are delayed due to the unavailability of key employees
- Interview decisions are delayed
- Hiring Managers are procrastinating around making offers

Human Resources and Talent Acquisition (HR/TA) are the departments that have direct contact with job candidates. If you suspect that there's a problem with your hiring process, engage them. Make them a valuable partner as you work to fix your company's broken hiring process. Encourage them to share the good, the bad, and the ugly of your hiring process. They should be able to share all types of experiences with leadership without fear of retribution. Recruiters within your company are also a key link to external talent. They present viable candidates to hiring managers for consideration. Recruiters are aware of the challenges, delays, and inefficiencies caused by a broken hiring process. They are charged with building relationships with candidates—establishing rapport and building trust. That's why they are often the first to hear candidate frustrations. The candidates often tell the recruiters about the lack of feedback and poor communications they experience. They complain to the recruiters when interview invitations are not extended to them in a timely manner. When offers take months to materialize, they vent to the recruiters about being left in limbo for extended periods of time.

If you want to bring about change in your organization, you'll need to engage your leadership team. After all, they are ultimately the people in charge of the company's organizational chart and shaping its culture. There are many contributors to a broken hiring process and many stakeholders who would benefit from fixing recruiting and hiring problems. To some degree, you need to involve all of the company's stakeholders. A broken hiring process is often a sign of a broken workplace culture. The more stakeholders who can identify hiring problems and create solutions to fix your broken hiring process, the more likely you are to achieve substantive results.

If you find that your hiring process is broken, you're not alone. At a minimum, most of you will find major inefficiencies. Many of you will find a recruiting and hiring process that is completely shattered. This leads to slow hires, candidate abandonment, or the wrong hires. According to a study by Leadership IQ, a global leadership training and research company, 46 percent of newly-hired employees will fail within 18 months, while only 19 percent will achieve unequivocal success. Let's take a deeper look:

> The study found that 26% of new hires fail because they can't accept feedback, 23% because they're unable to understand and manage emotions, 17% because they lack the necessary motivation to excel, 15%

because they have the wrong temperament for the job, and only 11% because they lack the necessary technical skills.

While the failure rate for new hires is distressing, it should not be surprising: 82% of managers reported that in hindsight, their job interview process with these employees elicited subtle clues that they would be headed for trouble. But during the job interview, managers were too focused on other issues, too pressed for time, or lacked confidence in their interviewing abilities to heed the warning signs.

Studies like this make it clear that the hiring process is broken at many companies. Unfortunately, the damage caused by this broken system also very expensive. According to an article by Peter Cappelli in the May/June 2019 issue of *Harvard Business Review*, "Hiring talent remains the number one concern of CEOs in the most recent Conference Board Annual Survey; it's also the top concern of the entire executive suite. PwC's 2017 CEO survey reports that chief executives view the unavailability of talent and skills as the biggest threat to their business. Employers also spend an enormous amount on hiring—an average of $4,129 per job in the United States, according to Society for

Human Resource Management estimates, and many times that amount for managerial roles—and the United States fills a staggering 66 million jobs a year."

BAD CANDIDATE EXPERIENCES HAVE A PRICE

You don't need to be embarrassed when you discover that your company's hiring process is broken. In fact, it's a cause for celebration. It means you've decided to face the music and fix the problem. Some companies go decades without acknowledging that their hiring process is broken. Instead, they lean heavily on their brand and name recognition to compensate for the problem, often facing irreversible damage to their reputation over time. Leaning on your brand too much and for too long—without fixing the underling hiring problem—is a dangerous strategy. Reputation and brand are fleeting. Candidates may recognize your company's name as a result of your marketing and advertising efforts, but this doesn't mean they feel an affinity toward your organization.

A bad candidate experience can severely damage a company's reputation, especially among the small but savvy pool of exceptionally talented candidates. How a candidate interacts with your organization provides a glimpse into your company's culture. Candidates will form their own opinions through their experience inside your hiring process. A bad reputation around candidate experience can cost your organization thousands or millions of dollars each year. Why? Because a broken hiring process will keep top talent from applying for positions with your company. Talented jobseekers will communicate their bad experience with their colleagues, friends, and professional networks. Add in the power of social media, and these negative reviews travel at warp speed. Over time, this negative feedback loop will ultimately trump your brand messaging. The outcome of all this unfavorable word-of-mouth chatter won't be pretty—or easy to reverse.

Creating a great candidate experience and an authentic professional culture where employees can thrive is foundational to every company's efforts to build an attractive brand that will rise above the noise in today's competitive talent marketplace. So how can you repair your broken hiring process? As I mentioned earlier, start with a fact-finding mission. Form a committee of all stakeholders inside your organization, and include HR/TA. Identify where the challenges are in your processes and discuss how they can be mitigated going forward. Implement a plan with commitment and ownership to ensure those same challenges do not appear in your organization again. Make the solution part of your culture. An exceptional hiring process should simply be part of the way you do business. It should be embedded into the very DNA of your organization.

YOU DON'T HAVE TO GO IT ALONE

If you're trying to orchestrate change and not seeing results, your company can also hire a consultant—someone like me who specializes in assessing, augmenting, and repairing broken hiring processes. A consultant will often provide you with more candid and direct feedback than an employee because there is no fear of retribution when they are candid about your company's problems. As a consultant, I am hired to tell the truth, no matter how hard that truth may be for my client to hear. I go into companies with an understanding that I'm going to be candid and direct. I'm there to rip off the bandage and show everything the problems that are festering and hurting their company. Employees don't always feel comfortable stepping on toes. That's why a lot of people sit on their knowledge. They see the problems, but don't make any noise about it because they are afraid of losing their jobs. A consultant can get to the truth of the matter.

The good news is, you can fix your broken hiring process and put your organization back on a path toward becoming an employer of choice. You can reclaim your great reputation and excellent candidate-experience reviews. Most importantly, you can jump-start growth with a more effective hiring process.

It is all up to you, but you don't have to go it alone.

Create an experience that will excite and engage your job candidates. Create a candidate experience that people will want to share with their friends, colleagues, and professional networks. Get candidates talking about your company in a positive way. Once you have created a hiring process that you can be proud of, you'll notice many key benefits. Productivity will increase, attrition will decrease, employee morale will flourish, and additional revenue and growth opportunities will become available. You can't achieve these things without a strong foundation, so make it a top priority to fix your company's broken hiring process.

CHAPTER 2
HUMANS ARE NOT WIDGETS. THERE WILL BE HIRING MISTAKES.

"Some of the best people we've ever hired
didn't seem to fit in at first, but proved
to be indispensable over time."
– Sir Richard Branson, founder of Virgin Airlines –

Since the beginning of my career as a recruiter, I have watched hiring managers battle anxiety in the face of hiring decisions. They either procrastinate, schedule too many interviews with a candidate, or require the consensus of every person down to the custodial staff before extending an employment offer. I am exaggerating just a bit, but you get my point.

In 1995, just before I graduated from Virginia State University (VSU), a historically black college and university (HBCU) located in Petersburg, Virginia, I was hired by an up-and-coming temporary staffing company headquartered outside Baltimore, Maryland. The company also had an office in Richmond, which was only thirty minutes away from VSU. It was an easy relocation opportunity for me and looked better than moving back to my hometown of Elizabeth, New Jersey, which was nearly six hours away.

I was assigned to the company's information technology division to help recruit highly technical talent to support our client base. The first customer I supported was a large paper company that needed candidates for a software implementation with an aggressive timeline. The software was fairly new, so there were not many candidates in the area with enough experience or proficiency to fit the job requirements. It was clear from the start that this was going to be a challenging assignment. Back then, Richmond was not an information technology hub—although that was changing quickly with large companies like Capital One choosing to establish their headquarters in the city. As recruiters, we had two choices: either recruit viable candidates from Richmond's limited tech talent pool or try to convince qualified candidates from outside the state to relocate away from tech hot spots like New York and California—a tough sell.

The client's hiring manager for the project was named Helen. She was respectful and fair, but very direct—a no-nonsense kind of person. I really liked her work style. You always knew where she stood. We worked well together. When I submitted a candidate to her for consideration, she would respond quickly as to whether they were qualified or not and let me know if she wanted to bring them in for an interview.

My recruiting partner Dave and I were initially frustrated because our candidate submittals were not hitting the mark. The candidates lacked the experience Helen needed. Dave and I worked day and night to find qualified candidates. We even worked weekends to try and build some momentum for the upcoming work week. After a few grueling weeks, we finally had a breakthrough. We were able to identify a good batch of candidates through advertising and referrals. We submitted three candidates to Helen, and she immediately agreed to bring them all in for interviews.

The three candidates were interviewed back-to-back on the same day. I called Helen before the close of business to get her feedback and determine if she was ready to make any hires. She told me that all three candidates were qualified and felt they would be great additions to the project and company. I was extremely excited.

"Can we begin having employment offer discussions with the candidates?" I asked.

"Not yet, Jermaine," Helen said. "I would like to see some more candidates."

I was disappointed and surprised, to say the least. Typically, if a candidate is qualified and the hiring manager says the candidate would make a great addition to the project, then an employment offer is expected. Helen had said great things about all three of our candidates but was not ready to make an offer to even one. I was perplexed.

"Helen, are there any issues with any of the candidates that I need to be aware of? Is their compensation a challenge or a project setback?"

"No, we are well prepared. I would just like to see more candidates before making any offers," she told us.

I did not press any further. Dave and I renewed our search for more viable candidates.

It took us a week, but we were able to find two additional candidates. Helen agreed to interview them both, but the exact same scenario occurred.

"They are well qualified and would be great additions to the project, but I would like to see a few more candidates," Helen told us once again.

At this point, I was becoming pretty frustrated. Dave and I had done a great job. Our boss Tim agreed. He wanted to arrange a meeting with Helen to understand her real concerns. Helen agreed and met us at a coffee shop near her office. Tim let me take the lead in the discussion.

"Helen, is there anything different I should be doing to find you candidates that you feel would be eligible for a hire?"

"Absolutely not," she responded. "You and your team have done an amazing job finding qualified candidates who have the direct experience we need and seem like they would be a great cultural fit for the organization.".

I was truly at a loss for words. I looked at Tim for some guidance, and he chimed in. "If we've done such a great job, Helen, why aren't you ready to extend employment offers to any of the candidates we've sent you?"

Helen paused and took a deep breath. "The project is extremely critical. It's the largest and most expensive project we have in the company. And it has visibility right up to the CEO. I can't make a mistake. I can't hire the wrong people."

She also mentioned that she had to present a weekly briefing to the executive leadership team on the project's health. This was when the light bulbs went off for us. Helen was suffering from selection anxiety due to the pressure and visibility of the project. She was paralyzed by the fear of making a hiring mistake. We explained what we were seeing and expressed concern that she might be suffering from selection anxiety.

"You're probably right," she responded.

CANDIDATE SELECTION ANXIETY IS REAL

Helen's story is quite common. Throughout my career in Human Resources and Talent Acquisition, I have worked with hundreds of hiring managers inflicted with candidate-selection anxiety. For Helen, the light bulb came on during our conversation at the coffee shop. She finally realized that she was the bottleneck in the hiring process. Once she confronted her candidate- selection anxiety, she could take action and start hiring. From that moment on, Helen worked alongside my team and me, and we were able to make the important hires that she needed to make. But what might have happened if she didn't have that light-bulb moment of self-realization? The problem would have lingered, and the company would have suffered as a result.

The fact is, hiring mistakes are unavoidable. Humans are not widgets. There are no perfect candidates or employees. If you are a hiring manager, I guarantee you that you will make a bad hiring decision from time to time. There is no quality control process that you or your organization can implement to prevent these bad hiring decisions completely. It's just life in the people business.

Having hired thousands of candidates myself, I can tell you that I have made plenty of mistakes. Some candidates who interview exceptionally and appear to be fantastic employee material turn out to be completely the opposite. On the other hand, candidates who interview poorly or do not have relevant experience can turn out to be some of the best employees and go on to achieve great things in their careers. Hiring talent is a risk. There is no foolproof hiring system. Personally, I just had to learn to trust myself enough to give candidates a chance to prove me right or wrong. That is the essence of the hiring process—allowing a candidate the opportunity to learn and grow with an organization.

To get over selection anxiety, you must learn to trust your hiring process and your instincts. Sometimes you just have to go with your "gut." However, if your hiring process is broken, you will make mistakes more often. Why? Because you don't have checks and balances in place to show you that you are making a mistake and how to correct it. If you put a solid hiring process in place and learn from past mistakes, I am certain you will have more success stories to share than failures. But you can save yourself a lot of stress if you accept the fact that you will not be 100 percent successful with your hires.

Procrastination and avoidance are not a productive way to handle selection anxiety. They only prolong the pain and ultimately hurt your company, and often your career. Trust me, indecisiveness causes bigger problems in the long run. I've seen those problems first hand. When you put off important hiring decisions, the work you are hiring to support remains incomplete- stress mounts. The only way to help overcome the challenge is to hire the experienced talent needed to get the job done efficiently and effectively. Additionally, if you delay the decision to hire for too long, candidates may begin to form a negative impression of your company as a "phantom employer"—that is, a company that gets candidates all excited about an opportunity but never makes a valid employment offer. Would your company benefit from this type of reputation? Absolutely not. Over time, negative impressions from candidates get spread around and start to erode your company's brand.

STRATEGIES TO COMBAT HIRING INDECISIVENESS

As I mentioned, waffling on hiring decisions can be bad for your career, too. Senior executives may begin to question your ability to lead and manage critical projects. Your current team of direct reports will continue being overworked and may look for opportunities outside the organization—even with your competition. Great talent is extremely hard to replace, and it is awfully expensive. Attrition is one of the highest costs to a company's bottom line and reputation. Finally, the stress, anxiety, self-doubt, and negative perception of your ability as an effective hiring manager may cause you to begin considering leaving the company or the HR industry altogether. Nobody wants to see that to happen.

Here are a few strategies I have used to combat hiring indecisiveness throughout my career:

- Create a hiring scorecard
- Invite team members to be part of the interview process
- Trust your knowledge and instincts
- Stop second-guessing yourself. You were given the authority to make hiring decisions because you have earned that authority.
- Accept that you will hire the wrong candidate in your career more than once. It's okay!
- Learn from your mistakes.

If you follow this guidance and embrace the realities of hiring talent, it will become part of your continuing development as a successful hiring manager for many years to come. It's important to accept that there are parts of the hiring process that you won't be able to control. There are many moving parts when you are dealing with people—especially when you are dealing with people from both inside and outside an organization. You won't be able to unearth every possible scenario when you make a hiring offer, so don't be so hard on yourself if something goes wrong. Don't take your hiring failures too personally. Some hires just aren't going to work out, despite your best efforts. Once you get used to this fact, the pressure will lighten, and your confidence will grow. Besides, if you have a streamlined, effective hiring process, you can compensate for that loss with timely new hires. There are things you can't control in the hiring process. It's no one person's fault; you have to be able to accept that and follow through. There are, however, a number of things you *can* handle in the hiring process. Learn to control and master those skills and learn to mitigate mistakes through positive actions grounded in a stellar hiring process.

CHAPTER 3

HOW CAN YOU DIFFERENTIATE YOUR COMPANY?

"The most meaningful way to differentiate your company is to do an outstanding job with information."

– Steve Jobs, co-founder of Apple –

The job market is changing fast. Candidates today are focused on more than just position, title, and compensation. These days, they are also interested in the health of a company's corporate culture, the company's stance on major social issues, work-lifestyle balance, remote work opportunities, how the company values its employees, and more.

Simply put, candidates are pickier these days about the organizations they join. And being pickier is easier than it used to be. Today's top talent has many online assessment tools at their fingertips. Research is easier than ever. Almost everything a candidate wants to know about a company is only a couple of mouse clicks or social posts away. This plethora of tools allows candidates to separate the wheat from the chaff. If they're sought after as a candidate, these tools allow them to be highly selective in their employment choices.

Companies face other complexities in today's job market. The size of a company no longer offers the competitive advantage it once did. Small, medium, and large companies all now compete for the same talent pool. This wasn't the case a decade ago. Today, many candidates aren't as focused on joining large organizations as they once were. They view larger companies as very bureaucratic and feel these companies will make it more difficult for them to have a voice—and having a voice is important to today's candidates.

Kyle, a former colleague of mine, a vice president of talent acquisition at a large government contractor, decided to start a technical services firm with two of his colleagues. The firm was supporting US-government contracts, and his number one concern was how would he be able to attract top young tech talent in a market where the government didn't have much credibility as an employer.

According to the May 14, 2020 issue of *Government Executive*, "Only 3 percent of tech employees working for the government in March 2018 were younger than 30, and only 14 percent of government tech employees were older than 60. As next-generation technologists chase their dream jobs at Facebook and Google—where the median employee age is 28 and 30, respectively—the gap will only worsen."

Kyle knew he had no distinct competitive advantage with regard to size or attractiveness. As a new player in the industry, his company couldn't rely on name recognition. He also faced other substantial challenges. He was seeking highly specialized candidates who also needed to have a security clearance. This meant that a number of his big-name competitors had an advantage over him. Kyle had to get creative and think outside-the-box about how to set his firm apart from the competition.

He decided to establish his firm as an employer of choice in his industry. To achieve this, he pushed his organization from the inside to do everything in its power to become an amazing place for top talent to work. He pledged to treat every employee he hired better than they would be treated at other companies. This not only meant providing better compensation and benefits, but it also meant offering richer employee engagement and more team-building events, among other things. These were all perks that would resonate with the talent market and give his employees to share with friends and former colleagues to help get them interested in Kyle's organization.

I thought that Kyle's plan was brilliant, and his hard work on this initiative paid off. Three years into building his company, it was officially named one of the best places to work in the state of Virginia. That kind of recognition is likely to get the attention of senior executives at small, medium, and large companies. This very public credential has

put his company on the map and has become a key compo-
nent of their marketing and advertising strategies. Today's
top talent is looking for organizations like Kyle's—organizations where they feel like they can be part of a company's
success and treated very well.

Kyle was ahead of his time; he gave his company an
advantage in a highly competitive talent marketplace.
Interestingly, he didn't go after some of the more tangible
perks as his differentiator. He took a people-focused approach, and it worked. Why? Because he thought about the
talent that he needed to reach to fill his jobs. He thought
about what corporate characteristics these candidates would
value, then he built a company devoted to those characteristics and values. He made his company look like the perfect fit
for the top talent he needed, and he pursued the credentials
necessary to document and publicize this fact.

GET CREATIVE ABOUT YOUR COMPANY'S DIFFERENTIATORS

Finding those things that will differentiate your company
from your competitors is key to hiring success. Whether
you try Kyle's approach and strive to become a "best place
to work" or try to stand out in some other area, the key is
to stand for something that attracts top talent. Perhaps you
offer a particular certification or training in your industry
(like the ISO 9,000 Quality Management Certifications).
Maybe you have a robust employee referral program or a

cool and quirky culture. You could even take a stand on social injustice or diversity. Whatever you do, choose something that will resonate with the talent pool that your company needs to reach, attract, and hire.

Your company's differentiators may be found in the most unlikely of places. Consider this fact: According to a study by *CEO Magazine*, Only 37 percent of employees indicated they were satisfied with the level of gratitude expressed to them at work. However, 96 percent of employees responded that gratitude in the workplace is either "somewhat important" or "very important" to them. Now, there's an interesting opportunity. Is your company really great at showing gratitude? If so, perhaps this is a core company value that you could convey to top talent.

Here's another idea: LinkedIn research indicates that 93 percent of employees would stay at a company longer if it invested in their careers. Additionally, 86 percent of millennials say they would remain at their current position if it offered more career training and professional development. But since these perks are not happening in a large sector of the professional sector, perhaps you could attract top talent by letting the world know that your company *does* develop its people and hires from within.

According to the Glassdoor Diversity Hiring Survey, "a full two-thirds (67 percent) of active and passive job seekers said that a diverse workforce is an important factor when evaluating companies and job offers." If diversity is important to your top talent pool and your company has a diverse and inclusive workplace, then this might be the place to start. We'll be talking more about diversity hiring in the next chapter.

Gratitude, career development, and diversity—these are just three ways you might be able to set your company apart in today's competitive talent marketplace. There are plenty of others, as well. As a hiring leader, you need to sit down and devote some time to creative thinking about your competition, your company's core values, your organization's position in your industry, and your ideal candidates' interests, desires, and current perception of your company. Remember that during this assessment process, you should focus your attention on the things that you can control. It's highly unlikely that you can suddenly change your company's size to become the biggest in your sector, so don't make size a differentiator. That's not something you can control. Instead, get creative, like my friend Kyle did. You'll be surprised by what you can uncover. Even your hiring process can become a differentiator. Build relationships with candidates and treat them with respect.

IS YOUR COMPANY WILLING TO ADAPT?

Don't sit on your hands and wait too long for your company to develop its position in the talent marketplace. Be proactive. Get creative. The talent your hoping to attract is not going to wait around for your company's brand to evolve. They are looking at companies that are already in the game, organizations that have committed the resources, time, and internal talent necessary to move their organization forward. These organizations are adapting, and they will thrive and grow as a result. Is your company willing to make a commitment to adapt? Let's hope so because you can't ride this one out. The strategies that worked in the seventies, eighties, and nineties will not work today. You have to listen to what your talent pool is saying. You have to listen to the changing times. You have to listen to your people. You have to be willing to commit your time and resources—and your organization's time and resources—to the process of identifying those unique qualities and perks that you can leverage quickly to attract and successfully recruit today's top talent.

There has to be more concrete, visible evidence of your company's commitment to the issues that are facing the world today. You have to get the knowledge base. You have to do the research. You have to ask the hard questions, and you have to implement a strategy that's sustainable over time. What will not work anymore is checking off some box for shareholders, staff, or leadership. What will not work anymore is an environment where your people feel like they can't contribute honestly to this important work for fear of retribution. This has to be a series of honest conversations among *all* key stakeholders—both internal and external to your organization.

As we all know, it's very expensive to replace talent that you've trained over several years. It's also hard to attract new talent to an organization that doesn't clearly understand its core values and differentiators. If that's the case where you work, then that's where the change must begin. Focus on things that will truly set your organization apart—not just from a compensation and benefits standpoint, but even from a time and community standpoint, like the more people-oriented approach that Kyle took.

Once you've decided on your differentiators, then it's time to figure out how to get the word out. You'll need to understand how the talent marketplace currently sees your organization and its brand with the key differentiators that you want to highlight. Chances are, you're not going to find the alignment that you hope to find, and you're going to have to discover creative ways to change this reality. It's difficult but important work.

There is truly no right or wrong way to differentiate your company. The only real mistake is to ignore the problem altogether. That's how your hiring process and growth can stagnate. Once you have identified your company's differentiators, all the stakeholders in your hiring process need to know how to consistently articulate crucial new messaging about those characteristics that help your company stand out. This messaging has to permeate every aspect of your hiring process—from advertising, press, and other talent outreach all the way through the recruiting, interview, and onboarding processes. Imagine if everyone who engages with your target talent is driving home your differentiators. Additionally, as they say, what if they're actually "walking the talk" with an effective and streamlined hiring process that shows candidates that your company lives by the core values it's communicating to the world. Now, *that* has the power to transform a company's growth trajectory.

CHAPTER 4

DIVERSITY HIRING IS SIMPLY THE RIGHT THING TO DO.

"Diversity and inclusion, which are the
real grounds for creativity, must remain at the center of what we do."
– Marco Bizzarri, CEO of Gucci –

As I mentioned in an earlier chapter, I started my career in the mid-1990s with an up-and-coming staffing agency headquartered just outside Baltimore, Maryland, and with several offices across the country. The agency's team was very homogenous—made up of a lot of Type A person-alities, many who had been high school or college athletes. They were mostly clean-shaven, well-groomed Caucasian men who wore single-breasted suits and drove American cars. Everyone knew each other because they were all either friends, relatives, or classmates who had referred one another to their first position at the agency.

On my first day of work at the agency's Richmond, Virginia office in June 1995, I arrived at 8:30 am, eager to begin my career. I was greeted by Peter, the Director of Business Operations (DBO). He was a serious, stocky former baseball player who was all business. As Peter showed me to my cubicle, I noticed there were no other faces that looked like mine. Even the female receptionist in the lobby was white. I became uncomfortable and anxious. I was out of my element. When I was at Virginia State University, an historically black college and university (HBCU), all my peers looked like me, talked like me, and had similar backgrounds. I knew how to act and fit in at VSU. I could be myself. Now, I was in an environment with complete strangers, and it didn't look like I was going to have much in common with any of them. I was a fish out of water.

After finishing my first day, I didn't want to return. My friends and family listened and were very supportive. I remember telling one of them about how self-conscious I felt when trying to pronounce the word "ask," and it kept coming out as "ax." At VSU people didn't call me out on this because we came from similar backgrounds and had similar ways of speaking. In my new job, though, this was not how people spoke. I seriously considered calling Peter and telling him I was no longer interested in the job. There were other opportunities; I felt I could land another position quickly. I wanted to run away. This feeling is common for minorities, women, and other ethnic groups when they begin careers in non-diverse organizations. The fear of being ignored or ridiculed is strong because there is no one else at the company that feels relatable.

Luckily, I did not leave. The first six months were extremely difficult, but I persevered and ended up staying for nearly four years. I was promoted after my first year and had great individual and team success during my tenure. Many of my colleagues were instrumental in my professional growth. They valued diversity and inclusion as much as I did. Interestingly, the company started hiring more diverse talent because I began referring my friends from VSU and other HBCUs. Many of my referrals excelled and developed into exceptional leaders, some who stayed with the company for more than twenty years.

ACHIEVING DIVERSITY IS DIFFICULT, BUT CRUCIAL

Here's the reality: homogenization is self-perpetuating. People hire others who look, think, and act like they do. It's comfortable. It's easy. If a company's leadership has no intentional strategy to become diverse and inclusive, it's just not going to happen. The uniformity will continue, and that will have negative consequences over time. Today, diversity and inclusion are critical components for success, growth, and longevity. Actionable commitment to diversity and inclusion sends a signal to the talent market about what your company truly values. Inaction sends a powerful message, too, and it's not positive.

There have been entire books written about the importance of diversity and inclusion in the workplace, but I want to take a moment to discuss some of the most important reasons. Why? Because from where I sit as a hiring consultant in today's competitive talent marketplace, a diverse workforce can no longer be an aspirational, long-term strategic ideal. Your leadership team can't think of diversity and inclusion as something they *hope* will happen. Today, the diversity of your workforce is a key growth driver and talent attractor. It can define your company's culture and success. Here are some of the top reasons why diversity should be a priority at your company:

- **Enhanced Creativity and Innovation.** The diversity of your employees creates the pool of perspectives into which your company's leadership can tap. If everyone on your team looks and thinks alike, how will you identify new products for market segments that don't look, think and act like your team? You're probably not. How are you going to solve complex human problems with homogeneous thinking? You're probably not. The more diverse your company's makeup, the more innovative it becomes. People come from all walks of life and bring their unique experiences, challenges, and solutions. This can become a big advantage to companies over time. In a May 27, 2019, Deloitte article entitled, "How and when can culturally diverse teams enhance team creativity and innovation?" researchers looked at 44 studies covering work by 2,832 teams and found that "Deep-level diversity in culturally diverse teams is positively related to team creativity/innovation." Deep-level diversity involves differences in deeper attributes among team members with different cultural backgrounds. How does this impact a company's bottom line? A study by the BCG Henderson Institute in Boston found that companies with more diverse management teams have 19 percent higher revenues due to innovation.

- **Improved Brand Reputation**—Diversity not only engenders goodwill among consumers, but it also allows your customers to see that your company "looks" like them. As a result, consumers feel that your company understands them better and your products and/or services become more relevant to them. This works for both business-to-business and business-to-consumer companies. This sense of being understood drives purchase decisions in powerful ways. We want to work with and purchase from companies that understand our problems, needs, and desires.

- **Heightened Sensitivity.** If your products, services, policies, marketing, or advertising messages are coming across as insensitive or out of touch, you probably lack diversity at your company. A diverse workforce nurtures empathy and a heightened sensitivity that permeates all aspects of a company, from products and services offered to policies, culture, and marketing and advertising messages. When you are more in touch with your buyers, your revenue grows.

- **Consistent Compliance.** Diversity hiring is especially important for companies that engage in federal contracts. If you can't meet a contract's hiring requirements around diversity, you might not land (or be able to keep) key government contracts. This can have a major impact on your bottom line, especially if a big portion of your revenue is devoted to government contracts. It can also prevent your company from exposure to potential discrimination lawsuits.

- **Faster Growth.** "According to a McKinsey report, executive teams that rank in the top 25 percent for being ethnically and racially diverse, are likely to reap financial returns of nearly 33 percent," wrote Pallavi Dhawan, director of Human Resources at Dun and Bradstreet India, in the June 2019 issue of *Entrepreneur.*

- **Avoid Negative Consequences.** Discrimination lawsuits failed ad and marketing campaigns, bad reputation with consumers, and the talent market—these are just a few of the negative consequences that you can avoid if you create a plan to make diversity and inclusion an intentional business strategy for your company.

Evidence to support these and other benefits of a diverse, inclusive workforce just keeps mounting. A study by the *Harvard Business Review* found that in a diverse company, innovation revenues can increase by one percent by nurturing the teams, two percent with respect to industry origin, 2.5 percent with respect to gender, and 3 percent with respect to managers with different career paths. The World Economic Form now says, "The business case for diversity in the workplace is now overwhelming."

Similarly, in a January 2020 article in *Forbes* entitled, "Diversity Confirmed to Boost Innovation and Financial Results," Stuart R. Levine wrote, "Diverse and inclusive cultures are providing companies with a competitive edge over their peers. This quote summarizes conclusions from *The Wall Street Journal's* first corporate ranking that examined diversity and inclusion among S&P 500 companies. The *Journal's* researchers' work joins an ever-growing list of studies by economists, demographers, and research firms confirming that socially diverse groups are more innovative and productive than homogeneous groups."

HIRING FOR DIVERSITY REQUIRES AN EFFECTIVE STRATEGY

In an ideal world, a diverse workforce means you employ people from many genders, races, religions, socioeconomic and cultural backgrounds, and abilities. Additionally, areas of study, industry background, career path, veteran status, and foreign work experience can be considered in shaping a workforce that is diverse. Growing and nurturing this type of workforce takes time and rock-solid planning and execution. It ultimately means you must prioritize inclusion as part of your company culture. However, when I look most companies' problems, the solution begins with a hiring and onboarding process that effectively identifies, attracts and nurtures diverse talent.

Even with good intentions, though, there are a variety of reasons that many companies find it difficult to get started or make significant progress toward their goal of creating a more diverse workforce. Things start to fall apart during the recruiting period. There might be problems with your ability to identify diverse talent, write an effective job description. There might be intentional or unintentional biases in your interview process when it comes to diverse hiring. Salary negotiations might not hit the mark, or other flaws in your hiring process might lead to friction and candidate dissatisfaction.

As a hiring manager for most of my career, I often encountered other hiring managers who had no idea about how to address their organizations' diversity hiring challenges. They knew that their company's diversity hiring numbers were abysmal, but only made attempts to correct them at the direction of HR and senior leadership. In other words, the hiring for diversity was not part of the company's culture.

"How can I hire more women and minorities?" is a question I have been asked often by hiring managers. To be helpful, I would create a strategy and share information regarding the approaches I have used. As a technical hiring manager, I would often send a list of associations the company should engage with like HBCUs with top accounting or engineering programs, the Society of Black Engineers, or the Minority Women in Technology. Most of the time, nothing ever happened as a result. These hiring managers would just sit on the information and dust it off each year after it became a topic of discussion and a casual concern of leadership yet again. It is a cycle and culture that exists within thousands of companies today. We must do better. The world is changing rapidly, and companies must change, too.

I've had my own struggles over the years with communicating and implementing effective diversity hiring programs in organizations that did not truly value diversity. It was always very frustrating and disheartening. America is a melting pot, and I have tried vigilantly to help change the culture surrounding diversity within several organizations–both as a consultant and as a member of the company's executive leadership team. I have hosted diversity and inclusion events, virtual diversity job fairs, diversity café gatherings where employees can bring in a dish from their culture to help educate the employee population. Nothing seems to work or stick long enough to have an impact.

A culture of diversity must start at the top of the organization and filter down through every department until it is ingrained in the company's DNA. This can't be forced; it must be nurtured by the leadership team. There must be a clear strategy and a plan to execute. There must be timelines, as would be required for any other important business initiative.

The country is going through a historic shift regarding race relations, civil unrest, social injustice, discrimination, and intolerance. Respect for different genders, sexual orientations, races, people from different backgrounds, and socioeconomic groups are coming together to help rid our society of systemic racism, classism, and unfair treatment of our citizens. This includes corporate citizens or employees.

The spotlight has been turned on, and it is exposing our nation's ugly, long-term challenges with diversity, inclusion, and unfair hiring practices. I've been advising my current clients and prospects to take a very hard look at their corporate culture. If diversity and inclusion are not key characteristics, it's time to do better! EEO (Equal Opportunity Employment and AAP (Affirmative Action Plans) are vital to ensure a company is addressing its diversity challenges and focusing on the population segment that hasn't been engaged in employment opportunities within an organization. It's time to take a scalpel to your EEO and AAP initiatives, identify areas that need help, and create a plan to fix them immediately.

The problems we have around diversity and inclusion weren't created overnight, and they won't be fixed quickly. But, just like anything else, until the problem is acknowledged and accepted—and the tough questions are asked—the same archaic and dismissive/avoidance behavior around diversity and inclusion will continue to persist and never be repaired. Let's make sure that doesn't happen. The stakes are too high.

DIVERSITY AND INCLUSION AS HIRING DIFFERENTIATORS

The business and economic case for diversity and inclusion continues to strengthen. Improvements in performance, growth, innovation, and more are all supported by a growing body of data on the topic. Inclusive companies with gender, ethnic, and cultural diversity continue to outperform companies lagging in this area. McKinsey & Company have been at the forefront of research in this area. Their 2019 study, "Diversity Wins: How Inclusion Matters," found that "... companies in the top quartile for gender diversity on executive teams were 25 percent more likely to have above-average profitability than companies in the fourth quartile—up from 21 percent in 2017 and 15 percent in 2014. In the case of ethnic and cultural diversity, our business-case findings are equally compelling: in 2019, top-quartile companies outperformed those in the fourth one by 36 percent in profitability, slightly up from 33 percent in 2017 and 35 percent in 2014."

Yet, progress is still slow for most companies. Though research on the clear benefits of inclusion and diversity continues to mount, progress in most industries has lagged—and therein lies an opportunity. As I said earlier in the book, creating a more diverse and inclusive workplace isn't easy. It takes a concerted effort, strategic planning, and buy-in from stakeholders across the company. That's not a simple thing to pull off.

Therefore, those companies that *have* fast-tracked their diversity and inclusion hiring initiatives have a key competitive advantage in the *Talent War!* Their diversity and inclusion initiatives provide an important differentiator that they can showcase to attract top talent.

According to *The 2018 Yello Diversity Survey*, "Companies that can demonstrate a clear commitment to diversity and inclusion will have a competitive edge in their recruiting. Why? Employees consider diversity part of their ideal workplace. Four of every five employed American (82%) consider diversity a part of the ideal workplace."

How do you signal to potential candidates that your company is committed to a diverse and inclusive workplace? An article on the LinkedIn Talent Blog, "5 Ways to Show

Candidates Your Company is Committed to Diversity," offered some great ideas, which I support and will paraphrase here:

- Showcase the diversity and inclusiveness of your existing workplace by posting employee photos on career sites, your website's career page, and elsewhere. Don't use stock photos as they might backfire.

- Similarly, let your current employees share positive stories about their experience working at your company. This is an authentic way to spotlight your workplace culture and its emphasis on inclusion and diversity.

- Bringing underrepresented candidates into an interview process run by a homogenous group of employees will only demonstrate that your company is not walking their talk. If you want underrepresented candidates to feel welcome during the interview process, it has to consist of diverse interview panels. According to the LinkedIn article, "In 2014, Intel began requiring that interview panels for all new hires include at least two women and/or members of underrepresented communities. Since then, Intel's diversity numbers have shot up. Before the new requirement, 31.9% of new hires were either women or people of color; two years later, they were 45.1%. Another upside of diverse panels is that they help decrease unconscious bias in the hiring process, which can be a huge barrier to increasing diversity."

- Employee resource groups (ERGs) were another strong recommendation in this article. These groups encourage underrepresented employees to help each other with some of the unique business challenges they face. They also advocate for improved inclusion and diversity policies within organizations. Talking about your company's ERGs—or better yet, including and ERG member on your interview panels—is a great way to show job candidates your company's commitment to diversity and inclusion. According to the article, "ERGs have been tremendously successful at companies like Walgreens, where several networks of employees (from veterans to members of the LGBT community) work together to advocate for diversity in recruiting, employee development, community engagement, and more. These networks have translated into meaningful wins for Walgreens. Its Disability Inclusion Network helped the company develop internal disability-inclusive technologies and policies, leading to a 100% score on the Disability Equality Index (DEI)—and attract disabled talent to the company."

- Finally, the article encouraged companies looking to hire underrepresented candidates to recruit at educational institutions with diverse student bodies and invite candidates to company events so that they can have real-world experience with your employees and the diverse and inclusive workplace culture where they work.

Over time, these small changes can greatly impact your company's ability to tackle homogenization and nurture a diverse and inclusive workplace that can attract top talent, which clearly values these corporate characteristics.

CHAPTER 5
RIP OFF THE BANDAGE! YOUR JOB POSTINGS NEED WORK.

"I choose a lazy person to do a hard job, because
a lazy person will find an easy way to do it."
– Bill Gates, founder of Microsoft –

When I am contacted by a prospect who is struggling to fill position or multiple positions, the first thing I ask to see is their list of job postings. Often, the problem is poorly written job descriptions. They are either too vague, too long, lack coherent details, combine multiple positions, or leave out key information necessary to attract the right kind of candidates. An effective job description is a critical part of a successful recruiting and hiring process.

The consequences of an ineffective job description are numerous. Poorly written job postings can cause your company to attract and hire the wrong candidate. This, in turn, can lead to higher turnover rates. One survey found that one-third of new hires left their job after only six months. That's a shocking number, and it has major financial, human, and brand implications.

There are many places where a job listing can go wrong. Here are a few:

- The job requirements in the listing are vague.
- The job requirements in the listing are not aligned with the type of talent you need.
- The salary or benefits are not clearly articulated.
- The job posting includes dated information about your organization.
- There's nothing about your company's key differentiators and corporate values.
- The job post is too general with language like "must be able to handle high stress environment" or "must be able to multi-task and work independently."

Let me share a story to show you how these types of problems manifest in the real world. In 2017, I received a consultancy referral from a Vice President of Talent Acquisition at a large technical government contractor. A startup had just won a large contract to support a new program at the Department of Defense (DoD). This was a multi-million dollar customer and a flagship win for the company. The startup had a team of recruiters ready to fill the positions, but they were having an extremely difficult time identifying, attracting, and recruiting the highly specialized candidates they needed.

My contact at the startup was Nancy, head of Human Resources and Program Operations (such dual roles are common in small companies). Nancy had a major problem to manage, and she had to find a solution quickly. The customer, a U.S. government agency, was threatening to file a cure notice, which meant her company was not performing to the terms of the agreement between the two organizations. The startup needed a plan of action to turn things around quickly. A cure notice is a public document that candidates and competitors can view. No company wants a public document showing failure to deliver. It labels the organization as a nonperformer. It's bad news for any company, but if you're a startup or a new player in the space, it can be a death knell.

Losing any part of the revenue from this contract would also have been catastrophic for Nancy's startup. It would result in layoffs or possible closure of the company. Needless to say, Nancy was incredibly stressed and anxious about her company's ability to finish filling the required positions. At the time of our engagement, more than 50 percent of those positions were unfilled and had been open for more than 60 days. More than 30 positions had aged so badly that the customer began sending some of them to other firms for additional recruiting assistance. Nancy and others at the startup felt a cure notice from the DoD was imminent. I asked Nancy why she thought the positions were remaining open for so long?

"Jermaine, there is just no available talent out there," Nancy told me without hesitation.

She went on to explain that candidates were simply not applying to her company's job postings on the corporate website or paid job boards like Monster, Indeed, and others. I was intimately familiar with the problems Nancy and her startup's recruiting team were facing. Intuitively, I knew poorly written job descriptions were the root of their issues. I had seen it too many times in my career.

A bad job description will grind your hiring process to a halt! If a candidate does not know what the company is looking for, he or she won't review your job posting with interest. The candidate will quickly move on to another posting that more effectively outlines the skills, experience, and characteristics required. I asked Nancy if my team could review the 30 most problematic job postings so I could provide her with direct feedback about the quality of the writing in the postings, the accuracy of the titles, the clarity of the required skills, and so forth. She agreed.

The next day my team started our audit. Almost immediately, we discovered the main problem. The position titles were highly cryptic and were not resonating with top talent. Assimilation Designer, Autonomy Administrator, Hardware Signal Chief were a few job title examples. Even we were perplexed by what these job titles meant. My team and I spent the next 48 hours retitling each job description so it would align more directly with the position's description. The job titles needed to more clearly and accurately communicate what the job actually entailed. In their current state, these job titles weren't attracting any candidates, even those actively looking for an opportunity.

I submitted our findings to Nancy with data to back up our new job title suggestions. We even provided her with sample resumes of candidates in the market that would be viable for each of her company's thirty positions. Nancy was blown away—and more than a bit upset that she or her recruiting team had not caught this major problem themselves. Had the startup not made this job titling error, it would probably have avoided the problems it was now encountering with its largest customer. I suggested that all the incorrect job postings be removed from the company's website and external job boards immediately.

My team replaced those job postings with updated title positions and waited to see if new candidates would begin to apply. In less than five hours, new candidates began applying. The recruiters were able to start screening more candidates. The hiring managers were excited to interview more job seekers and ultimately extend employment offers. Within ten business days, there was eight employment offers extended and accepted. Nancy and the leadership team were ecstatic. The client was pleased with the increased hiring productivity and stopped threatening a cure notice. Nancy's crisis was averted—all due to more effective job titles.

When we do a client audit at my firm, JLW Management Consulting, we follow a strict protocol driven by the following principles. You can follow these principles, too. They will help you write more effective descriptions to attract top talent to your job opportunity:

- **Follow the Data.** It was clear when we looked at the numbers that Nancy's startup was experiencing a problem at the beginning of the recruiting process. The issue wasn't about a slow interview process or candidates rejecting job offers. Her company just wasn't attracting enough applicants. Bottlenecks can happen at any stage in the recruiting and hiring process, so follow the data for clues. Once you spot the problem, address it quickly.

- **Analyze Your Processes.** Nancy's startup was struggling because it didn't have the proper systems in place to write and test effective job descriptions. With our many years of experience, we were able to see the problem quickly. Still, most companies— especially startups and younger organizations— don't have proper workflows in place to recognize job posting issues before they blow up and cost a company time, money, and reputation. Analyze your hiring processes to identify and fix problems before they get out of hand.

- **Get Feedback Recruiters & Candidates.** Put together a list of targeted questions for your recruiters and candidates (both those who joined your company and those who didn't). With list in hand, have someone on the management team regularly reach out to get specific feedback about your job descriptions, scheduling process, interview experience, recruiter-candidate communications throughout the hiring process, and your onboarding process (if applicable). It's time-consuming work, but the information you gather can be invaluable, ultimately saving your company precious time, money, and resources.

Poorly written job descriptions—with vague titles, lack of key information, or sloppy writing—are among the main reasons candidates don't apply. If you have systems in place to prevent this problem or address it early when a job posting has an issue, the number of applicants for your positions will increase exponentially. This sets your recruiters and hiring managers up for success. If you don't have enough applicants for your unfilled positions, conduct an audit. Identify the issues with your job postings and correct them quickly. It will save your organization time, money, and a ton of headaches. We all know how unfilled positions can impact a company's reputation and bottom line, so if your organization is struggling to attract the right talent, start by looking at your job descriptions.

CHAPTER 6
YOU DON'T NEED TO INTERVIEW
10 CANDIDATES.

"My biggest mistake is probably weighing too much on someone's talent.... I think it matters whether someone has a good heart."
– Elon Musk, Founder and CEO of Tesla Motors –

ood people are your organization's lifeblood. They drive revenue, breathe life into your company's brand, drive innovation, and build your company's future. That's why attracting and hiring the strongest candidates is so important. But the typical hiring process is time-consuming, expensive, and stressful for everyone involved. Common hiring-process inefficiencies only magnify these issues.

One of the biggest inefficiencies in the hiring process is at the top of the interview funnel: initial candidate selection and first interviews. New technologies and job marketing platforms have made it much easier to attract large numbers of candidates to a job posting, especially if the posting is written in general terms and not designed to detract unqualified or ill-suited candidates from applying. More candidates might sound like a good thing, but it can be a curse.

"The typical employer will interview 6-10 candidates for a job," according to the website careersidekick.com, "and candidates will go through at least 2-3 rounds of interviews before receiving an offer. If a hiring manager isn't able to find someone who fits their requirements in the first 6-10 candidates, they may interview more." Yet, according to *Harvard Business Review's* Recruiting Spotlight Series in May-June 2019: "Recruiting and hiring consultants...estimate that about two percent of applicants receive offers." That seems like a lot of wasted energy. The article goes on to say:

> "Unfortunately, the main effort to improve hiring—virtually always aimed at making it faster and cheaper—has been to shovel more applicants into the funnel.
>
> Much better to go in the other direction: Create a smaller but better-qualified applicant pool to improve the yield. Here's why: Every applicant costs you money....Every application also exposes a company to legal risk, because the company has obligations

to candidates (not to discriminate, for example) just as it does to employees. And collecting lots of applicants in a wide funnel means that a great many of them won't fit the job or the company, so employers have to rely on the next step of the hiring process—selection—to weed them out... [and]...employers aren't good at that."

I couldn't agree more! When it comes to picking initial candidates to bring in for job interviews, less is more. Reverse the quantity-over-quality mindset that dominates your company's initial candidate selection. It's nothing more than overcompensation for inefficiencies elsewhere in your hiring process (poor job descriptions, a weak interview process, selection anxiety, etc.). Bringing more candidates into a broken hiring system won't fix anything; it will only compound your problems.

GOODBYE TO THE "MORE-CANDIDATES-ARE-BETTER" MENTALITY!

As a consultant, I confront the more-candidates-are-better mentality all the time. The first thing I do when I'm brought in as a consultant and meet a team with this mindset is to demonstrate that a smaller pool of more viable candidates can actually speed up the hiring process and save the company valuable time, money, and resources. Flipping to a *quality*-over-quantity approach also leads to better results. I have many case studies to back up this statement. My work with a hiring manager named Bob serves as a perfect example to demonstrate my point.

Bob hired me to find and engage viable candidates for a single, important position that he needed to fill. My goal was to send Bob a nice selection of qualified candidates and do so as quickly as possible. My team and I had a several in-depth conversations with Bob to identify the type of candidates he wanted to interview. We started the job, and things on our end were going well. We were able to identify a pool of great candidates. Bob was pleased. Those candidates were moving through the interview process efficiently—another good sign. In a week, we had submitted thirty viable candidates to Bob. That's quite an accomplishment. But Bob did not make one interview decision. After seeing all those candidates, he still wanted to interview more people for a single position. Does that sound like an efficient process to you? Is it really necessary to review that many candidates in order to make an interview selection and, ultimately, the right hire? No, it's not. Having to interview that many candidates is a clear sign of a broken hiring process. Bob ultimately filled the position, but he could have done so in half the time, sweat equity and at half the expense. Don't make this mistake at your organization, especially if your talent requirements are at scale. Just think what Bob's hiring experience would have looked like if he had thirty or sixty or a hundred positions to fill. What a stressful, ineffective and inefficient hiring situation that would be!

DON'T DRAG YOUR HEALS WHEN HIRING

You don't need Google, Monster, Indeed, or any other online job-position marketing site to get the right person into your hiring funnel. You simply need targeted cold calling by people who know your specific requirements for a viable candidate. As we discussed in earlier chapters, not understanding your specific requirements for a job is one sign that your hiring process is broken. To do their job well, recruiters need proper direction. How else can they establish whether a candidate is a good fit for an interview? No recruiter—no matter how experienced—can single out viable candidates for your position without clear criteria to guide the selection process. If you can't provide solid guidance, you don't have a strong foundation for your hiring process. As a result, you will probably not achieve the desired results.

Those on the front lines of the hiring process—recruiters and hiring managers—also need to know that your HR team is willing to move fast once they've identified top candidates. The top talent you seek is not waiting around for your sluggish interview process to kick in or your offer to arrive after several months of back and forth. Top talent typically has interest from several of organizations. This means that when they're ready to move to a new position, they can move fast. If you drag your heals, you'll lose them. I've seen this happen over and over, especially at companies that frontload their hiring process with dozens of candidates.

My team worked with a hiring manager name Andrew in the manufacturing sector. He was having trouble meeting his hiring requirements and called us in to help him fix the problem. Andrew needed a constant team of high-quality talent to fill positions in a scaling company. Initially, Andrew thought his problems stemmed from a lack of qualified talent. This is a common excuse my team hears. It's just easier for people to look outside the organization and identify problems. Looking inside Andrew's hiring process, however, we began to see the company's real problems. Andrew and his team had plenty of qualified candidates—and because they had a more-candidates-are-better mentality, they wanted to see a lot of candidates. But because Andrew was bringing a high volume of candidates into an inefficient hiring process, he set himself up for failure. His organization lost candidates right and left all along the way due to the inefficiencies of their hiring process. Scheduling interviews took forever. Getting approvals to hire from HR took even longer. Candidates just got fed up and looked elsewhere— and rightfully so. Top talent typically has choices, so it behooves your company to talk with fewer candidates and move them through the hiring process quickly. Andrew's company was doing exactly the opposite, and it was creating huge problems for his organization.

It's difficult to understand why hiring managers feel that they need to see thirty candidates to make a hire, especially when a similar result can be achieved with fewer candidates—typically five or seven candidates would suffice. If you're on a hiring team, I can't emphasize strongly enough the need to shake this quantity-over-quality mentality. It just doesn't work. Not only will it clog up your hiring process and erase any efficiencies you might have achieved, over time it will crash your entire hiring system and hit your company's bottom line—hard. There's just no way to hit hiring targets when you have a high volume of candidates and a broken hiring process. It's a lethal combination. Interviewing too many candidates, especially without weeding out those ill-equipped for the job, is a waste of your company's time, money, and resources. It can damage your organization's brand in today's open and competitive job marketplace, where people can post about their experience with your company's drawn out and frustrating hiring process.

THE ANTIDOTE TO YOUR HIRING PROBLEMS

The antidote to this type of destructive chaos is simple: write a clear and accurate job description that will empower your recruiters, and hiring manages to find a few good people who fit the bill. If you're unsure what a great job description looks like or how to assess the key criteria for a candidate, then return to Chapter 5 for a refresher because fully understanding this concept is key to your success. Articulating what your company needs in a position is crucial to the success of any hiring process, but it's especially important when you want to narrow the pool of candidates earlier in the hiring process. But once those requirements are nailed down, you can empower your recruiters and hiring managers to weed out the wrong candidates early, conduct fewer interviews, assess those candidates quickly with an effective interview process, and make your offers in a timely manner. You'll save your company valuable resources and prevent a lot of headaches. It might seem counterintuitive, but you have a better chance of hiring the right person from a smaller pool of well-vetted candidates than you do from a larger pool of poorly screened people.

If you're skeptical about this approach, take a look at some of your key hiring metrics: What's your company's time to hire? What does it cost your company to fill a position? What does your new employee retention rate look like? What do your recruiters think about your hiring process? How do candidates view your interview and hiring experience? If you're bringing a ton of candidates into your recruiting funnel and your answers to these questions are discouraging, then maybe it's worth trying something new. Here's what a less-is-more approach to hiring looks like: Well researched, well-written job descriptions are prepared to attract top talent into the hiring process or maybe well-prepared recruiters with a strong understanding of the job requirements and company culture cold call. Either way, top talent applies. Hiring managers then weed out those candidates who are not a good fit, and five to seven candidates—the cream of the crop—are invited into the interview process.

Interviews should be scheduled quickly and run efficiently. Candidate follow-up communication is clear and timely. Offers are made quickly, and candidates who did not make the cut are thanked for applying. Onboarding begins. The process is continually monitored for efficiency and effectiveness around a clear set of key performance indicators. When problems arise, they are addressed quickly. Opportunities for improvement are always encouraged, which means the corporate culture is one that respects and values the opinions of its people on the front lines of the *Talent War!* That's what it looks like to have a quality-over-quantity hiring philosophy baked into your company's DNA. And I can tell you from my many years of experience watching companies transition from quantity to quality when a company's hiring process runs like a well-oiled machine, the entire organization benefits.

CHAPTER 7

ARE YOUR MISSION, VISION, AND VALUES A CULTURAL PRIORITY?

"If you hire people just because they can do a job, they'll work for your money. But if you hire people who believe what you believe, they'll work for you with blood and sweat and tears."

–Simon Sinek, author & speaker

M ission. Vision. Values. Talk to any corporate leader or management consultant today, and you'll hear these buzzwords roll off their tongues. These concepts have become ever more popular over the course of the last decade because a growing body of research has revealed that "meaning is the new money"—an idea coined in a March 23, 2011, *HBR* article by Tammy J. Erickson, a top 50 global business thinker that year. What's behind her statement? Some mind-blowing numbers around how mission, vision, and values create a culture of meaning that translates into more productive and engaged employees.

Seven years later, *HBR* asked a team of thought leaders, "How much is meaning worth to an organization?" On November 6, 2018 the published the following:

> "[E]mployees who find work meaningful experience significantly greater job satisfaction, which is known to correlate with increased productivity. Based on established job satisfaction-to-productivity ratios, we estimate that highly meaningful work will generate an additional $9,078 per worker, per year.

> Additional organizational value comes in the form of retained talent. We learned that employees who find work highly meaningful are 69% less likely to plan on quitting their jobs within the next 6 months, and have job tenures that are 7.4 months longer on average than employees who find work lacking in meaning. Translating that into bottom line results, we estimate that enterprise companies save an average of $6.43 million in annual turnover-related costs for

every 10,000 workers, when all employees
feel their work is highly meaningful."

Those are some impressive numbers! It's also one of the reasons why communicating your company's mission, vision, and values to job candidates are more important than ever. Clear articulation of these three important concepts can play a central role in attracting top talent and having candidates accept job offers from your organization. It can help you entice the right kind of candidates to your job postings—those whose values are aligned with your company's mission and vision.

In the last chapter, we talked about diversity and inclusion as important core values that every company should strengthen in the twenty-first century. But there are many other types of corporate values. Here's a sample: Integrity, teamwork, collaboration, the pursuit of excellence, trust, respect, personal accountability, growth and happiness, environmentalism, equality, and so on. The mission, vision, and values of a company can be as diverse as the personalities in the workforce. Every company wants to be seen as unique. Nobody wants to work for a company that is generic.

VALUES ALIGNMENT IS KEY

Of course, it's key to ensure that your company's mission, vision, and values align with those of the candidates you need to attract to your organization. If you understand the values that your pool of top candidates find enticing, then these values become powerful leverage in the hiring process. That's not meant to sound forced; the goal is authentic alignment. However, if your organization's values are *not* aligned with your candidates' values, your company will have a very difficult time attracting, onboarding, and retaining the right type of talent. In other words, there will be far too many mismatches.

This is why it is important to have strong communication between your company's HR leadership team and the recruiters on the front lines of the hiring process. The recruiters have daily conversations with top candidates. They can see the trends and shifts first hand, in real-time. They have a lot of valuable information to share with the leadership teams, which is responsible for creating and translating corporate mission statements. If there's a clear channel for recruiters to communicate what's happening in the real world of potential candidates, then opportunities to "lean in" to the moment can be created quickly. Take, for instance, the recent uptick in candidate interest in flexibility and remote work benefits during the COVID-19 pandemic. If your company has core values around flexibility or health and wellbeing, there is a perfect opportunity to hone your values messaging in a way that resonates with today's candidates, and that messaging can be pulled right through to the types of benefits you offer job seekers. In 2020, 43 percent of full-time employees in the United States say they would like to continue working from home after the economy reopens. A permanent work-from-home policy could become a key differentiator for your company when talking with candidates. If you don't have a way to listen to what's happening on the front lines of recruiting, it's time to figure out a better way. You're missing out on crucial intelligence from the candidates your organization is interviewing.

The reality is, it's not always about wages for candidates. In fact, according to Glassdoor's Q3-2015 Employment Confidence Survey, 89 percent of 18-34 year old employees care more about great perks and benefits than they do about pay raises. What perks and benefits trump a pay raise? Trends indicate that today candidates are looking for perks and benefits that include: financial wellness, mental healthcare, student loan repayment, transgender-inclusive healthcare, technology benefits, family planning, flexible schedules, commuter benefits, paid leave, remote work, and even pet benefits. In the best of circumstances, these benefits are closely aligned with your company's core values. Are you listening to the candidates you want to attract and hire? Do you know what they value, and are your values aligned with theirs?

DOES THE WORLD KNOW ABOUT YOUR MISSION OR CULTURE?

Even if you have the greatest mission with the best perks, benefits, and culture in the world, it's practically meaningless if no one outside your company knows anything about it. We see companies fall in this area all the time. The disappointing part of this communication breakdown is that the leadership team has done the hard, strategic work to define their mission, vision, and values—they have built a strong foundation for meaningful corporate culture—but they have failed to let the outside world know anything about this important work. There's no brand messaging on these amazing attributes of their organization, and that's a huge mistake.

Mission, vision, and values should guide a company's culture, and these days candidates care a great deal about corporate culture. According to builtin.com, "A strong company culture will attract the right candidates for the job and keep them engaged as employees. According to a recent Glassdoor study, 77% of adults would evaluate a company's culture before applying to an open position. Perhaps more impactful, 56% rank an organization's company culture as more important than compensation."

If your organization is failing to effectively articulate your mission, vision, values, and culture to the outside world, here are some ideas to turn that around:

- Include specific core values in all your job postings.
- Share your company's mission statement with candidates.
- Interview candidates in a space where they can experience your company's corporate culture.

- Create value-driven questions and statements for your interview process.
- Develop candidate nurture campaigns with an emphasis on your company's mission, vision, and values.
- Ensure your company's mission, vision, and values are part of all brand messaging to employees, candidates, and the media.
- Include value-driven messaging on your website and career sites.
- Empower your employees to share the company's mission, vision, and values on social media.
- Make sure your values are incorporated into your benefits packages, and that connection is clearly articulated to candidates.
- Share stories and statistics about your company's mission, vision, and values with job candidates and make sure everyone on your hiring team is aligned in the way they discuss these topics with candidates.

STRATEGIC PLANNING FOR THE RIGHT CULTURE

So if mission, vision, and values are key drivers of growth—on both the revenue and people side of an organization—then why haven't more companies taken concrete actions to focus their culture on the creation of meaning? This is ultimately an assignment for the company's leadership team— who must then effectively permeate their message throughout the organization—but it takes intelligence, data, and inputs from a variety of stakeholders: HR, executive management, middle management, employees, hiring managers, recruiters. In other words, it takes a lot of collaboration and coordination to get it right. It requires an integrated approach. It also takes a senior leadership team that understands that culture, mission, vision, and values are key growth drivers that should be at the forefront of strategic planning.

In a March 28, 2019 article entitled, "Strategic Planning That Strengthens Your Culture," author Stuart R. Levine wrote:

> "Not every senior leader thinks about their strategic planning process as an opportunity to enhance their organizational culture. However, your culture is the key to moving the needle on revenues, and every opportunity to enhance it also enhances the opportunity for financial return. Smart leaders use the planning process to create more engagement within the workforce, and to increase leadership capacity. An effective strategic planning process generates trust and enthusiasm at all levels of the organization . It is data-based and

fosters broad ownership with accountability. It is about strengthening the team to work together in an inclusionary and focused way....

Successful strategy is founded on your mission, vision, and core values. The planning process develops and clarifies critical drivers and gives voice to the organization's value proposition upon which the strategy is based. This iterative process brings new candor to the executives' interactions and embodies the values of listening and collaboration. It means that all participants engage with each other and share honest critical thinking. Everyone at all levels understands that their input matters, and their voices will be heard. Openness and inclusion builds the trust that is fundamentally required for a healthy culture. Furthermore, the organization has an expressed goal to truly function as an integrated team."

From where I sit as a 25-year recruiting and hiring veteran, a values-and-mission-driven culture is not easy for companies to get right. In fact, a 2018 Gallup Poll says that 53 percent of workers say they are "not engaged." They may be generally satisfied with their work, but they are not cognitively or emotionally connected to it. They will show up and do what is required, but will quickly leave their company for a slightly better offer. If this is how more than half the workforce feels about their jobs—and Gallup interviewed more than 30,000 employees for this poll—then American businesses have a very long way to go. It's an unsettling reality with major consequences: "Organizations that are the best in engaging their employees to achieve earnings-per-share growth that is more than four times that of their competitors," according to Gallup. "Compared with business units in the bottom quartile, those in the top quartile of engagement realize substantially better customer engagement, higher productivity, better retention, fewer accidents, and 21% higher profitability."

The gap between what senior leadership teams believe their mission, vision, values, and culture to be and how a company's employees feel about their workplace culture is still huge. If more than 50 percent of workers say they are not engaged, this should serve as a wake-up call. This enormous gap is not only negatively impacting the bottom line of America's corporations; it's negatively influencing their ability to attract, employ and retain top talent...and as we all know, this does not set in motion a virtuous cycle for growth and innovation. Just the opposite.

It's time to ask yourself, are your mission, vision, and

values a cultural priority? If you can't answer "yes," then perhaps it's time to shake things up because the alternative is not sustainable. Change doesn't happen by accident. The very top of the organization must support the culture shift and effectively and continuously communicate it throughout the company. The messaging around the culture shift should also be channeled out into the world where tomorrow's employees—who are watching and listening—can see that your company's culture provides meaning every job it has to offer. The challenge of this undertaking is immense, but what's at stake is even bigger.

CHAPTER 8
WANT TO HIT YOUR REVENUE GOALS? HIRE FASTER!

"You can dream, create, design and build the most wonderful place in the world...but it requires people to make the dream a reality."

– Walt Disney –

I n 2018, a small healthcare analytics company in Virginia won and important contract with the US Army. The company did not have an interview or hiring process in place because it was so small. Most of their hiring up to that point had been through employee referrals or the owners reaching out to their professional network for recruiting support.

Since the positions for the new contract were niche, highly technical, and required a government security clearance, the company's casual recruiting methods were unlikely to be effective and would take more time than available to fill the jobs. When Susan, the company's Human

Resources leader, saw some of my company's marketing materials on LinkedIn, she sent me a message describing the urgency of their recruiting needs. She suggested we talk that very afternoon, even though it was late on a Friday.

On the call, she laid out her need to hire 60 candidates in six weeks to avoid defaulting on the new government contract her company had been awarded. This type of project was right up our alley. It required a quick ramp up, a scalable and effective hiring process, and scope—all in our wheelhouse. At the end of our Friday afternoon conversation, she said she wanted to get started first thing Monday morning. My company was able to stand up an entire recruiting organization over the weekend with a team of recruiters and recruiting administrators to manage the onboarding process that I had presented to her.

By implementing a robust, accountable hiring process for her organization, we met the required goal of 60 hires in six weeks. In fact, we exceeded the goal. I honestly believe it was because Susan fully supported our solution and rallied additional support from her company's C-suite executives. The company's leadership was united and onboard, and this commitment permeated throughout the organization. This level of support made it easier for us to align resources and build ongoing trust with the company's hiring managers. There is nothing more frustrating than trying to help an organization fix its problems while constantly facing resistance. It is extremely counterproductive, but unfortunately, all too common. However, with Susan as our champion, the barriers we often face as outside recruiters were virtually nonexistent. Susan and the leadership team's support was key to our ability to do our job and ultimately made this critical hiring project a success for her company.

We stayed on with the organization as an outsourced recruiting partner for nearly two years. During that time, we hired more than 150 new employees for them. Ours was a partnership based on trust and a history of performance. This combination eliminated potential bottlenecks and allowed us to streamline the onboarding process. The hires we made for the initial project resulted in tens of millions of dollars' worth of revenue the company—revenue the company might not have been able to realize had they not worked with an outside recruiting firm and supported their decision to do so at a senior level. After being awarded the contract, the company took decisive action and made a commitment to support my team. As a result, we were able to work together to significantly increase the company's bottom line and reputation.

Hiring an outside recruitment firm is a tough decision for some companies. It can create internal friction, especially if the company's leadership team does not champion the hired firm. Collaboration is key, and stakeholder buy-in helps the entire team—both the hiring managers within the company and the outside recruiters—follow the designed hiring process and achieve the defined hiring goal. When process without implementation and lack of execution creep and create roadblocks, companies can find it difficult to achieve their hiring goals.

WHAT'S AT STAKE IF YOUR HIRING PROCESS STAYS BROKEN?

Why does any of this matter? What is at stake if your company misses its hiring goals? The answer is a lot: revenue, productivity, innovation, top talent, company reputation, employee morale, and retention. A dysfunctional hiring process can have a negative impact on all of these areas, so there is a lot at stake if you don't hire quickly and effectively. Does that always mean you need to hire an outside recruiting firm? No. Does it mean you should consider it if you don't have the internal hiring capabilities to reach your hiring goals? Yes, it does. Wavering on that decision could cost you and your company dearly. In Susan's case, hiring an outside recruiting firm made the difference between losing a major government contract and earning tens of millions of dollars in revenue. It was an easy choice for Susan because she knew what was at stake if she didn't hire top talent fast and efficiently. Because her company was small, she knew she needed outside help.

Why is hiring fast so important? How does a streamlined and efficient hiring process benefit a company? Let's take a closer look at this issue. HR thought leader Dr. John

Sullivan summed it up nicely in a June 3, 2019 article for <u>ere.</u> <u>net</u>, an online gathering place for recruiters. The article was entitled, "Recruiting's Top 7 Bottom-line Business Impacts That Most Ignore":

> "In today's highly competitive talent marketplace, making fast hiring decisions is more important than it has ever been. Faster hiring means you won't lose high-quality in-demand candidates who may be gone in as few as 10 days. Losing top candidates mean that you will be forced 'to settle' for second choice candidates. That will lower team productivity because in some cases, the second-choice candidates will perform 20 percent less than the No. 1 candidate....
>
> Slow hiring means that key unfilled positions are open for dozens of unnecessary days. And with no one in the job, obviously, the work remains undone. The productivity or revenue loss for some jobs may be several thousand dollars for every position vacancy day. And because many time-to-fill days are 33 percent too long, the lost productivity can be tremendous. The strain of team members having to fill-in

for vacant positions may also increase team stress and turnover."

Maybe you think that hiring slower allows you to assess and hire the best talent. In theory, that might sound logical, but in reality, the opposite is true. "The longer you take, the lower the quality (i.e. the "on-the-job performance" of new hires) will be," Dr. Sullivan continues in another <u>ere. net</u> article entitled, "The Top 12 Reasons Why Slow Hiring Severely Damages Recruiting and Business Results":

> "The primary reason for this drop off...is that with an extended hiring process, all of the top candidates will likely drop out, leaving only weak ones to choose from. Most managers don't realize that the secondary impact of having all of the top candidates drop out is that the remaining candidate pool...may now only contain average and weak candidates. As a result, the extra time for decision-making is negated by the fact that you only have average candidates to gather that information on. Unless you measure how quickly the quality of the candidate pool drops over time, you probably won't realize how damaging delayed hiring can be. You can easily find out how long it

takes before the top candidates drop out by first identifying the top 10 percent of your applicants and then periodically contacting each of them to see how many days pass before they move on (it is usually between 10 and 20 days). *The lesson to be learned is:* that slow hiring may actually doom your firm to an extended period where you only hire average or slightly above-average candidates. Recruiters may offer the excuse that the weak applicant pool that they presented is a result of the highly competitive marketplace, but in many cases the actual reason may be a slow hiring process that only exists at your firm."

While I've seen a fast and efficient hiring process contribute to the growth of many a company during my long career, I've also seen a slow hiring process damage growth, morale, innovation, and productivity at many other companies. It's difficult to watch hiring inefficiencies blossom into a company-wide meltdown. I've seen it happen all too often. That's why Dr. Sullivan's point about measuring Key Performance Indicators (KPIs) around hiring is so important. KPIs are the specific yardsticks you use to measure your success. Performance measurement is the only way to diagnose and stop the cancer before it spreads. KPI tracking is an excellent way to spot hiring problems at your company. Here are my top three hiring KPIs—notice that two of the three have to do with time efficiencies:

- **Time-to-hire.** Recruiters can determine time-to-hire by subtracting the date a candidate entered the hiring process from the date that candidate entered the hiring process, either through an applicant tracking system (ATS), referral, or some other channel. If the number of days it takes your company to make a hire is higher than the average in your industry, this could be a sign of trouble. If other companies in your field can fill a key position with top talent in two weeks and it takes your company two months, there is a major competitive disadvantage. The problem must be addressed quickly and thoroughly. Outside help to diagnose and treat the issue is probably warranted if your time-to-hire metrics are poor.

- **Time-to-fill.** This KPI captures the time for the entire hiring process, starting with the job requisition to job acceptance. It's a broader measure than time-to-hire, and can reveal inefficiencies at the beginning of the hiring process—even before the first candidate applies. This KPI looks at the times it takes to lay the foundation for your hiring strategy—the time it takes to determine the job requirements, the number of hires needed to meet strategic business goals, and the time it takes to write job descriptions and distribute them in the proper channels where candidates can start applying. When you add the time it take for these up-front hiring processes to your time-to-hire metrics, you'll have your time-to-fill number. The longer the time period identified, the lower your score, and the higher the stakes become to fix your broken hiring process.

- **Quality-of-hire**. This KPI is measured differently by individual companies and within different industries. It is a measure of the value a hire brings to a company. It's an important KPI because it can reveal key insights about your hiring process. Performance, productivity, and retention are common indicators used to determine the quality-of-hire metric. The data to calculate quality-of-hire often comes from performance reviews a few months after a hire is made. The easiest way to calculate quality-of-hire is to take the numbers associated with each indicator and add them together. Then, divide this number by the total number of indicators. That number is then multiplied by 100 percent. Consider what is revealed if high performers typically leave your company six months after hire. This might be a wake-up call to your hiring managers and recruiters that they've got to do a better job of screening candidates for cultural fit during the interview process. On the other hand, low performance by recent hires could mean your company needs to figure out why it's not attracting top talent or if there is a problem with your training and onboarding process. As you can see, the quality-of-hire metric can be a revelation. And since poor hiring processes and high turnover rates can be very expensive for companies, tracking this measurement is crucial.

Several other important KPIs are associated with the hiring process, but my experience has shown me that if the above three are weak, your company has a big problem that needs to be fixed quickly. It is often difficult to see complex problems from the inside of a company, especially in a growth phase when everyone is pushed to their limits. That's why measurement and quantifiable data is so important. It's often even more difficult to fix complex hiring problems without outside assistance, a topic we've discussed in previous chapters. When people think their criticism of the company's hiring process might cost them a promotion—or even their job—they tend not to be forthcoming. That's when bringing in an outside recruiting consultancy can really help a leadership team get to the heart of a problem, come up with viable solutions, and assist with the recruiting process until new hiring systems and processes are internalized by all key stakeholders inside the company.

HOW TO SUCCESSFULLY PARTNER WITH AN OUTSIDE RECRUITING FIRM

If your company does decide to work with an outside recruiting firm because you believe it will enable you to hire faster, more efficiently, and help you meet crucial hiring goals, here are some tips on how to make the partnership a successful one:

- Everyone in your company needs to be on the same page with regard to the hiring process and the decision to work with an outside recruiting firm. This means everyone from senior leadership to your internal hiring managers and HR needs to be working in harmony to support the outside recruiting firm that your company has hired.

- From the start of any project with an outside recruiting firm, success will require a well-articulated plan, clear communication of that plan to all stakeholders, and open channels of communication throughout the project.

- If you are heading up the project, you must decide which decision points require your input.

- Eliminate bottlenecks and make sure that your hiring team doesn't have "process paralysis." Having too many people involved in the interview process can delay the hiring and onboarding process. For example, make sure interviewers' calendars are aligned to avoid rescheduling and missed interviews and appoint people to conduct the interviews who can provide valuable input about the hiring decision.

- There must also be some level of autonomy in the hiring process. A company can't have seven people making decisions on a hire. Pinpoint one or two people who have the authority to make hiring decisions and let them work with the recruiting firm.

Hopefully, after reading this chapter, you understand why hiring fast is so important. Equally crucial is your company's ability to measure whether it is hiring quickly and efficiently compared to your competition. Much can be lost if you are not competitive in your hiring process. If you discover that your company has a broken hiring process, act quickly to communicate the problem to key stakeholders, and consider solutions immediately.

HOW HIRING IMPACTS BUSINESS HEALTH

Most of the content in this book is about improving your company's hiring process to attract and onboard top talent more efficiently and effectively. Within these pages, I've aimed to provide a plethora of ideas about how to diagnose hiring-process problems, improve results, and create a hiring system that can help your company achieve—and even exceed—its business goals. However, I only briefly touch on the close connection between hiring and the overall health of a business. The relationship is closer—and more crucial—than most realize.

This section will reveal the "why" behind your work. It will spotlight the reasons that recruiters, hiring managers, and HR leadership teams are so important to the overall health and performance of a business. A broken hiring process often signals bigger concerns at a company. Think of your hiring process as a health barometer for your business—it's a measure of overall well-being and future potential. A weak or ineffective hiring process often signals problems like dysfunctional workplace culture, stagnating revenue, or ineffective leadership. In other words, if your hiring process is broken, chances are several other strategic business levers are broken as well.

Talent has always been a driver of business growth, but now more than ever, winning the *Talent War!* is crucial. Why? Because today people change jobs much more often than they used to in the past. "According to careers-advice-online.com, "The average person will change careers 5-7 times during their working life according to career change statistics. With an ever-increasing number of career choices, 30% of the workforce will now change careers or jobs every 12 months. By the age of 42, you may already have had about ten jobs."

Today, unhappy employees can become job seekers in a matter of minutes. They have job-search and career technology at their fingertips. If someone is displeased with their current position or wants to change their career path, information and opportunities are just a couple of mouse clicks away. According to the *Harvard Business Review*'s May-June 2019 Recruiting issue, "...the majority of people who took a new job last year weren't searching for one: Somebody came and got them. Companies seek to fill their recruiting funnel with as many candidates as possible, especially "passive candidates," who aren't looking to move. Often employers advertise jobs that don't exist, hoping to find people who might be useful later on or in a different context."

These changes to the job marketplace have many important implications for companies. First, it has put enormous pressure on hiring teams and leadership, who must stay ahead of the turnover. HR is now asked to create a never-ending stream of new talent while shaping a workplace culture that retains employees for as long as possible. Second, the high cost of hiring must be managed in today's more fluid talent marketplace. The Society for Human Resource Management states that the average cost to hire an employee is $4,129, and it takes on average 42 days to fill a position. Those costs add up quickly, especially if a company has an inefficient hiring process. Finally, hiring managers and recruiters on the front lines of the *Talent War!* are forced to battle for talent on more fronts than they have in the past.

Since the war for talent is now relentless and continues to change at a more rapid pace than in the past, many companies are taking a more agile approach to HR and hiring—much like the agile development systems used by corporate technology departments. They are outsourcing duties to hiring firms with strong hiring processes and laser-focused execution. Internally, new skills are in demand. According to the same *Harvard Business Review* article, "The HR function will also require reskilling. It will need more expertise in IT support—especially given all the performance data generated by the new apps—and deeper knowledge about teams and hands-on supervision. HR has not had to change in recent decades nearly as much as have the line operations it supports. But now the pressure is on, and it's coming from the operational level, which makes it much harder to cling to old talent practices."

If you work in HR or as a recruiter or hiring manager, you face these new challenges every day. You are being asked to reshape and retool our industry, which should give new meaning and purpose to your work. From where I sit as a consultant, broken hiring processes seem to be the rule rather than the exception. Part of the reason for this is most hiring systems were built in a different time that had different challenges. Now it's time for an overhaul, a much needed update. The best people to conduct this overhaul are the people like you, who spend their days battling it out on the front lines of the *Talent War!* Yes, it is a daunting challenge to reshape an entire industry, but it's exciting, too. Are you up to the challenge?

CHAPTER 9

GUESS WHAT YOUR CANDIDATES ARE SAYING?

"If we weren't still hiring great people and push-
ing ahead at full speed, it would be easy to fall
behind and become some mediocre company."

–Bill Gates, co-founder of Microsoft

o you know what candidates are saying about your company during and after the hiring process? In today's era of social media, candidates are sharing their experiences with the world. They can provide instant feedback on social sites like Facebook, Twitter, Instagram, Glassdoor, Yelp, LinkedIn, and many others. Their social updates about your company—whether positive or negative—can go viral in a matter of moments. Is your company's HR department paying attention to what these candidates are saying? If not, it's a missed opportunity that will come back to bite you.

It's easy to dismiss candidate comments on social media.

We tell ourselves it's just a one-off from an unhappy person or that the candidate is just having a bad day and blaming us. Often, though, dissatisfied candidates speak the truth on social media. They are talking about real problems they have encountered while interacting with your company, and they are using social media to warn others based on their experience. Candidates expect companies to value their time, ideas, opinions, skills, and experience. Candidates don't appreciate it when organizations treat them poorly, take advantage of them, or waste their time. These candidates often have good reason to be disgruntled. In the past, however, it wasn't quite as easy to let the world know how they felt. That has changed dramatically. With the click of a button, millions can share their experience—good or bad—with millions more. Word of mouth has found a megaphone in social media, and this should be a wake-up call for your company's hiring team.

Having been in this business for more than 25 years, I have experienced the hiring process from every perspective. I've talked with thousands of candidates who have been through dysfunctional hiring processes that took too long and were filled with frustration. I've also been a corporate hiring manager and had to run terrible hiring programs weighed down by too many decision-making layers, too many people, bad processes, and poor communication. I've been part of leadership teams trying to fix their broken hiring process. I know just how hard that can sometimes be—given the bad habits, politics, and overall bureaucracy of many organizations. I've watched miserable hiring experiences impact both candidates *and* hiring managers, who have to deal with the fallout from their company's bad practices every day. Believe me, it takes a toll and negatively impacts a company's culture, reputation, morale, retention rates, and more.

IGNORE CANDIDATE FEEDBACK AT YOUR PERIL

There is a treasure trove of valuable information in candidate feedback, even if given on social media rather than through a more formal feedback channel. You ignore this feedback at your peril. Do you think that candidate who never heard back from your company after the first interview doesn't have a valid complaint? Do you think it's fair to leave candidates hanging because you don't want to tell them that they won't be invited for a second interview. or you won't be extending an offer? The avoidance approach is more common than you might think, even though it never works. When those candidates who have been left hanging take to social media to vent, is it possible that they have a valid reason? Yes, it is. Not having your recruiters follow up with candidates and provide them with prompt feedback leads to legitimate frustration. There should be no surprise when candidates leave negative social remarks. You showed them little consideration or respect so why are you surprised when they do the same?

In more recent years, I've been the consultant whose team was brought in to fix things, and I've had the opportunity to see transformation firsthand. When a hiring process finally starts to work efficiently and effectively, good things begin to happen. Candidates talk about this on social media, too, and that's a win. One of the reasons I decided to write this book was to bring this mix of perspectives to the discussion because *everyone* suffers when from a broken hiring process, and everyone *benefits* when it's fixed. If you see a stream of negative social comments about your hiring process, fix it fast. Here's how:

> **Listen.** Your company should try to mitigate negative candidate experiences—and as a result, negative candidate perceptions—around their hiring process. Someone on the hiring team—be it in HR or operations—should be assigned to monitor and review social comments and watch for patterns. They should be charged with capturing and distilling information from candidate social posts and reporting back to the organization so that problems can be fixed quickly. This and other information inputs should inform the design of a hiring process that ensures that each candidate has a favorable experience.

Gather. Hiring teams should actively seek candidate feedback from both rejected and accepted candidates. In other words, you can't always be reactive; it's better to be proactive. Capturing and learning from candidate feedback is an essential part of an effective hiring process. You want to know what's going well and not so well when it comes to candidates—no matter whether they were hired or not. In fact, it's probably more important to understand the experience of those candidates who were rejected. Think about it from a numbers perspective. You hire many fewer candidates than you interview for a position, so there are many more candidates talking about your company after they've been rejected than after being hired. Do you know what they are saying? Do you have a system to find out? I'm a big believer in formalizing the feedback process. It's a crucial part of any effective hiring system. Here's what I recommend: After an interview, communicate the next steps clearly and expeditiously. If a candidate is rejected, at least you don't prolong the pain and anxiety associated with waiting. This opens the door to follow up with a professional email and ask for feedback from that candidate. You'll always know where you stand with rejected candidates, and because the candidate feels "heard," he or she is less likely to write a negative post about your company on social media.

Plan. If you have been actively listening and synthesizing feedback from job candidates, you should be able to identify problems and see negative patterns. This information can help you form a plan to address those dysfunctions. Put together a plan and present it to your team. Show them that you've done your homework and demonstrate how the negative candidate experience—and accompanying negative social posts—are hurting the company. Try to quantify the damage whenever possible.

Execute. Take your plan, build support around it, and execute it quickly to stop the negative candidate experiences and social comments as quickly as possible.

Repeat. This should be an ongoing process, a discipline of your hiring team. It will create a virtuous cycle of continuous improvement, which will benefit all stakeholders in the hiring process and ultimately minimize negative posts about your company. You want your hiring process to create brand ambassadors, not brand killers.

It's worth noting that negative comments travel farther and faster than positive comments. It's just human nature; people tend to key in on bad reviews. According to a 2018 *Inc. magazine* article, "Dissatisfied customers typically tell nine to 15 other people about their experience; some tell 20 or more." This makes it very challenging to undo the damage. Once bad reviews or comments are out on social media, it's almost impossible to reign them back in. On some platforms, it's a sort of permanent record, forever tainting your company's reputation. Once something is out there in the world, there's just not much that you can do about it. That's why the goal is to mitigate candidate concerns early and make certain that your hiring process values candidates' time and talents—even if you don't hire them. This mindset should be communicated regularly to your hiring team until it becomes part of your culture. I promise you, this approach will not only change your company's outreach to candidates; it will have many benefits within your company as well. This same mindset can be carried over to exit interviews when an employee is leaving your company.

Listening respectfully to professional comments when an employee departs will help your organization improve and live up to its core values. Former employees will also leave with a sense of being "heard" and "valued," making it unlikely that they will rant about you on social media. If you walk the talk, people feel that your organization truly lives up to its core values—and that type of alignment is central to a strong brand in today's competitive talent market.

YOUR HIRING TIMELINE MUST BE SHORT

As I mentioned earlier in the book, in the mid to late nineties, I was the hiring manager for a very large product project located in Blue Bell, Pennsylvania. I worked out of the company's Richmond, Virginia offices. The project supported a large financial services organization based out of San Diego, California, with offices across the country and around the world. We were a startup with only about 50 employees at the time, and we were charged with hiring over 200 employees for this major financial services institution. One of the things we didn't quite understand at the beginning of the project was that we didn't have control of the hiring process. We were brought in to operate within an existing hiring infrastructure—unfortunately, it was very broken.

My manager's name was Scott. He was the account manager for this particular financial services company, so we flew to San Diego to meet with our point of contact Sheila. Our goal was to have an in-person meeting to explain how we would be able to support them in their hiring efforts going forward. We told them the number of resumes we would submit for their consideration. We talked about how we would handle reference checks, schedule interviews, and extend hiring offers. What we did *not* explain was what we needed from Sheila and her team in order to deliver on these expectations. That was a mistake.

We quickly learned that the company never really had a formal hiring process. The organization did most of its hiring via its website. It was a completely virtual approach with very little or no contact with candidates. The startup where Scott and I worked, however, was the exact opposite. We were very high contact. We talked to every candidate and screened them before submitting them to our clients. We scheduled all the interviews directly with each candidate and discussed salary expectations with them before our clients would be asked to extend an offer.

Our first task was to hire 50 financial services reps, also known as customer service reps. These were low-level positions. We had a lot of candidates applying to our job postings, and had spoken to many of the candidates prior to submitting them to our client. Scott even suggested we hold a hiring fair on the campus of our customer in San Diego. We were charged with doing all the marketing for this event.

We handled all the email invites, postings and advertise on our internal website. We also sent out invitations directly to viable candidates who we had identified.

About two weeks before the hiring fair was to take place in San Diego, we began to finalize everything. The goal of the fair was to interview as many people as possible during the job fair and make hiring offers on the spot. Two days before the event, Scott, I, and another recruiting partner flew out to San Diego. We went to our client's facility to map out the event space, which was going to be a large conference room. We mapped out the logistics and flow— how the candidates would come in, how they would move through the process, who they would speak with along the way, etc. We were methodical, and we were prepared.

The event was scheduled to start at 9:00 am and end by 3:00 pm. And at the end of the event, we would tell each candidate if they were coming back for a second interview or not. We would also make contingent offers on the spot based on select candidates' salary expectations and the budget we had for each position. The hiring fair went off without a hitch and was a great success. We saw more than 200 candidates—maybe 70 percent of them were viable. Most of the candidates who attended had prior customer service experience in the financial industry. They were very sharp, knew how the process worked, and presented themselves very well. Scott and I were psyched!

As time went on, we began to notice that some candidates were not given feedback on whether they were coming back for a second interview or whether they would be extended a contingent offer. Those who weren't a good fit hadn't received formal notification of their rejection. Most of the candidates were left in limbo. We started to feel like the whole job fair was just about collecting resumes. During our huddle up after the event was over, Scott and I looked at the 200 plus resumes we had collected. It was time to head back home to the east coast, and it felt like we were leaving all these people in limbo.

We flew home, and two more weeks went by with still no feedback. We tried to schedule a virtual call with our client but were given excuses: scheduling issues, people out of the office, travel plans, and other excuses of that nature. We hit the one-month mark and still nothing. We had more than 200 excited candidates, and instead of filling jobs, nothing had happened at all. I called Sheila to talk about all the great candidates we had waiting for them. We went through all the candidates again and made decisions on whether to bring them back for another interview, reject them, or make a contingent offer. I left the meeting feeling like we had made great strides, this project was back on track, and Sheila and her team were ready to move things forward. Two more weeks passed, and we weren't given the green light to make any offers or invite people back for a second interview. All the work Scott and I had done to help our client was for naught. We were working inside a broken hiring process that we couldn't fix. It was a painful but valuable learning experience. I wonder if you can guess what all those candidates said about their experience with our client. I don't think it was pretty.

CHAPTER 10

YOUR EMPLOYEES ARE GREAT! LET THEM HELP.

"No matter how brilliant your mind or strategy, if you're playing a solo game, you'll always lose out to a team."
– Reid Hoffman, cofounder of LinkedIn –

Your employees are your greatest recruiters. They know your organization inside and out. Often, they've been with the organization for years, sometimes many years or even decades. They understand your company culture. They believe in your organization's mission. They've navigated their careers within your corporate structure. If they've been with your organization for ten years or more, they are personally and emotionally committed to the company's future. They want to see your organization grow and thrive because they have contributed their time and talent to the organization's success thus far. It makes perfect sense for these invested individuals to help you identify, attract, and recruit your next group of top talent. Companies that tap their employees and incentivize them to refer job candidates typically reap many benefits.

According to a January 21, 2020 article in smartrecruiters.com, "…82% of employers rated employee referrals above all other sources for generating the best return on investment. Hiring teams looking to widen and diversify their talent pools via referrals can easily do so with an employee referral program (ERP)." The article lists the multitude of benefits associated with these programs—perks that I know well as a veteran recruiter. Here are some of the top benefits they listed:

- Increased Hiring Velocity
- Easier Access to Qualified Candidates
- Lowered Hiring Costs
- Better Outcomes

EMPLOYEE REFERRAL PROGRAMS REALLY DO WORK

I've seen the positive impact of ERPs firsthand over and over again. That's why I'm a huge proponent of these types of programs. Let me share a story to demonstrate. In 2014, I was promoted to vice president of talent acquisition for a large government contractor. They were having challenges hiring and attracting talent mostly because they were growing fast and had many openings to fill. With about 5,000 employees and 400 active job openings, I was brought into the position to get things moving in the right direction. In my first days in my new position, I met with Tom, the senior vice president of human resources, to understand what he felt the challenges were. Tom was a seasoned veteran. He had been in government contracting for more than 30 years. He had run HR organizations for some of the largest companies in the Washington, DC metro area. He was also extremely successful at change management—that is, turning organizations around with stronger, healthier cultures. I asked Tom what factors he felt were contributing to the low percentage of employee referrals within the organization. I wanted to understand how a company with 5,000 employees, where one would expect quite a bit of referral activity, had such a low percentage of employee referrals. Tom's answer was simple: He didn't feel the organization had done a good job creating an enticing employee referral program—one that would engage employees to contribute or refer their friends and former colleagues. I offered to take on the project to see if my team and I could help create a more attractive process to increase employee referrals, and Tom gave the green light.

The organization's recruiting staff was doing a great job filling open positions as quickly and efficiently as they humanly could; there were simply hundreds of openings to fill. As Tom and I both knew, employee referrals are simply the fastest, most effective, and most cost-efficient way to attract strong talent into an organization. It was time to fast track our ERP. At the point I took over the program, the employee referral rate was below 10 percent. Our goal was to increase that percentage to 15 percent within a year. To kick things off, I gathered my staff to talk about the challenges Tom and I had discussed. I wanted to gather their ideas and opinions about creating and structuring an attractive employee referral program. There was a pretty clear consensus around how to build an attractive ERP. My team suggested that an effective program must:

- Have an online portal that would make it easy for them to refer a candidate. It had to be user friendly for both employees and referred candidates.

- Provide feedback quickly to current employees and referred candidates. The wanted to know whether their referral would be interviewed or told he or she wasn't a good fit. They requested a clear channel for ongoing communication throughout the hiring process—and this was for both the referring employee and referred candidate. People hold their referrals near and dear to their hearts. They have a history with these people, a personal relationship. They did not want to refer someone into an organization that was going to waste that person's time, treat them poorly, or fail to provide effective feedback in a timely manner.

- Offer a monetary incentive. Employees felt that they should benefit from the impressive savings a company enjoys from an ERP. They suggested a bonus of $2,000 if a referred candidate was hired. This type of extra pocket money could help with unexpected expenses, holiday gift-giving, college tuition, or just a little more spending money. My team felt that this incentive would get current employees excited about contributing to the new employee referral program.

We put the program's details together in a little over a week's time, including all of the elements my team had suggested. I showed the plan to key people across the organization to gather their feedback and opinions. This is important because it created momentum for the project and secured "buy-in" from key stakeholders. This is always a crucial step in building support for a new company-wide initiative. I incorporated everyone's best ideas and expressed my gratitude for their input. Then it was time to take the program back to Tom. One week after our initial meeting, I met with Tom again and presented our new employee referral program. Tom and I discussed the program at length. He gave input on monetary incentives, portal implementation, and many other factors. Our mutual goal was to ensure that the program would roll out effectively and that the current staff would receive it well. I incorporated the majority of Tom's ideas into the plan. Tom gave the go-ahead, and we prepared to roll out the new ERP to the company's 5,000 employees.

I met with our marketing team to draft the initial communication documents for the program. The goal was to share the benefits and incentives of the ERP not only with those employees located in the Washington, DC area but all around the country, even those deployed internationally. The launch went smoothly,and within the first three months of rolling out the new program, we started to notice a dramatic increase in employee referrals. The incentives were working. On the front end, there were so many referrals being made through the online portal. We were worried that it could handle the volume. Thankfully, it worked effectively. On the back end, the recruiting staff did an outstanding job of communicating and informing the staff about their referrals. They let the referring employees know when their candidate was received into the portal, what stage of the recruiting process they were in, and what each candidate's next step would be. As promised, they gave constant feedback throughout the recruiting and interview process, all the way through to employment offer decisions.

Adding this new talent pipeline through the referral portal—along with our regular job postings on our website and other external sites—had an almost immediate positive impact on our recruiting efforts. Suddenly, we had more than enough candidates to review. We also added an intra-company site where employees could apply to be considered for positions internally. It was a big hit. People were excited. Very quickly, we went from a 9 percent employee referral rate to nearly a 25 percent employee referral rate. The company's leadership team was ecstatic. We paid out more than six figures to employees who had referred successful candidates. Our cost per hire was lowered because we didn't take a lot of time using outside agencies or waiting for candidates to apply through our traditional methods of job or website postings. We were able to get candidates in process faster, extend offers more promptly, and onboard our new hires quickly. These efficiency improvements, of course, had many benefits for the company. Revenue increased at a faster pace, and morale was at an all-time high, which helped our retention rates for current employees. We were able to hire some great talent that we wouldn't have otherwise been able to attract through normal methods.

A few months after the program's launch, I presented Tom with our impressive results. He was ecstatic. We were making more hires as a result of the new employee referral program. It was a huge success. A robust employee referral program makes it so much easier for current employees to refer their friends, colleagues, and relatives. It will always outperform traditional hiring channels in which recruiters must post job descriptions externally and wait for candidates to reply, which puts a lot of pressure on the recruiting team. The employee referral process is a vital recruitment tool. It's cost-effective. It's revenue-generating. It's morale-boosting. There aren't any disadvantages to having an effective employee referral program. Once you identify all the advantages and start to see the results, you, too, will realize that it's a key ingredient to any company's overall hiring success.

WHAT'S HINDERING YOUR ERP'S SUCCESS?

When I engage with a client or prospect who is having hiring challenges or needs to increase hiring numbers quickly, I often ask about their employee referral program. If they don't have one, I help them start one. If they have a program, and it's not working, I evaluate their incentives and communications and suggest changes. I sometimes even scrap the current referral program and build a new one. In every case over the last 20 years, when I have audited, changed, and implemented a new employee referral program, the company has seen tremendous growth in its hiring process with a lowered cost per hire. Morale had increased, and the company's retention rates have gone up because employees are able to earn extra income from their referrals. If your company needs to hire more candidates and faster, a robust employee referral program is the way to go.

There are a few scenarios where a well-constructed ERP can fail to achieve its goals. Typically, however, the failure has little to do with the actual program. Here are the top three scenarios I've seen that can hinder the results of an ERP:

1. **Your workplace culture is broken.** Why would your employees refer their friends, family, and colleagues to your company if they don't feel good about working there? If you want your ERP to succeed, you've got to fix your broken workplace culture.

2. **Your recruiters aren't communicating.** When your employees put their relationships on the line to make a referral, you recruiters better treat both parties like gold. This means stellar communication every step of the recruiting process to both the referring employee and the job candidate. If communication channels fail, your referrals will dry up fast and your ERP will be doomed. If you want your ERP to succeed, ensure clear, consistent and effective communication between recruiters, hiring managers, employees, and candidates.

3. **Your program doesn't have support.** I've talked about this problem before. Don't build your ERP in a bubble. Rather, gather support, input, and feedback as you build the program. Do this at every level in the organization—from senior leadership to employees in every department to human resources and your recruiters. It might take a little extra time,

but gathering this crucial support will help you build a strong foundation for your program. If your ERP to succeed, gather input, feedback, and support while you build it.

Liz Ryan, a Fortune 500 HR senior vice president, summed up the problem perfectly in a January 23, 2015, *Forbes* article entitled, "The Truth About Employee Referrals."

> "An employee referral program is a flame-y idea. When I say 'flame-y,' I mean that a successful employee referral program has a lot to do with trust and good feeling. There are mechanical aspects to the program, of course, but they are less important than the less measurable but more high-impact factors in your program's success.
>
> Simply stated, if the employees don't feel good about the place, they're not going to subject to their friends to the environment. What kind of friend does that?
>
> If your employees have submitted their friends' resumes in the past and have been blown off, or treated to a month of radio silence, ditto. Who wants to put up with that?

When your employee says to his friend, "Hey John, there's an opening in my department -- do you want to apply for it?" and John says, "Sure," your employee is on the line.

If your teammate can't give John some information within a week or so about what's happening with John's application, your employee is the one holding the bag. Your employee feels like crap and looks like a bad friend to his friend John. You can't put your teammates in that position! You have to make employee referrals fast and very responsive. You have to treat your friends' friends like gold.

Then again, I want you to treat all of your job applicants like gold. That's how you build community around your organization. That's how you cultivate evangelists. You make your workplace a great place to be. Recruiting is very easy then."

If your company has other problems it needs to fix—like a broken workplace culture or weak communication channels—is an employee referral program still really worth all the effort? My answer is definitively, yes. The truth is, you need to fix these problems anyway; they are already hurting your recruiting efforts. Additionally, ERPs are worth the effort for a multitude of reasons. These programs offer many benefits and have a very strong return on a company's investment of time, money, and resources. In this case, I will let the numbers speak for themselves. The following stats were found on recruiter.com:

- Companies that use employee referral programs have average retention rates of 46 percent, compared to the 33 percent retention rates of organizations that only use career sites.
- Referred hires start their jobs sooner than other hires. Candidates from career sites start after 55 days. Those found on job boards start after 39 days. Employee referrals start after only 29 days.
- Referred candidates are 3-4 times more likely to be hired than non-referral candidates.
- New hires sourced via referral programs produce 25 percent more profit for their companies than new hires sourced via other means.
- Referral programs can save organizations $3,000 or more per hire.

As I said earlier in this chapter, I've seen all these benefits and more firsthand in my long career. I've experienced ERPs benefits as a recruiter, a hiring manager, an HR executive, and more recently as a recruiting and hiring consultant.

Great people are always a company's most important asset. Tap into that asset to attract more great people. It's that simple, and it's one of the most powerful recruiting tools out there.

CHAPTER 11
OVERCOME YOUR FEARS AND
WIN THE TALENT WAR!

"The secret to successful hiring is this: look for
the people who want to change the world."
– Marc Benioff, CEO of Salesforce –

The management of human resources has always been a
tough job. HR personnel, hiring managers, and recruiters are on the frontlines of the *Talent War!* And since
attracting, hiring, and retaining the best talent is pivotal to
every company's success, the stakes are high—very high—
in our industry. With high stakes come high levels of stress.
It's just part of the job description. But it is important to
keep things in perspective. You can't let anxiety stop you
from forging ahead, facing challenges, and doing your job
to the best of your ability.

You can count on one thing in the hiring process: You
are dealing with human beings, so things will go right some

days, and things will go wrong other days. These ups and downs are part of the human experience, and thus part of your job in human resource management. It's important to accept—even embrace—this reality. Resilience needs to be a skill you develop. If you don't hone this skill, you're going to crack. Stop torturing yourself with the notion that you can control every variable when you're working with human beings. You can't. Accept this reality, and the ups and downs of your job will become easier to manage both emotionally and professionally.

Let's not kid ourselves, hiring the right person isn't easy. It has never been, and it never will be. Even with the introduction of artificial intelligence into the hiring process, there are still so many what-ifs. I could try to develop a specific number of variables that are in play when a candidate interviews for a job and feed that into an algorithm, but I'd never do justice to the complexity of that process. There are systems, processes, tools, and resources that can improve the hiring process, but nothing can make it foolproof. Even under the best of circumstances, mistakes will be made. The wrong person will be hired. The right person will be hired, but won't stay. Yes, your very public hiring project—which leadership has been watching for months—will hit road bumps that everyone will notice. That's why hiring anxiety is a real thing. Understand that most leadership teams grasp the fact that hiring doesn't happen in a straight line. They know that there will be bumps and curves along the way.

Your success will not be measured in perfection, but by how you handle the inevitable challenges that will occur in the hiring process.

It is important to remember that you are operating in a talent WAR. Battles will be won, and battles will be lost, but ultimately it's about winning the war. This is what matters, and it takes strategic planning and the ability to move forward even after a lost battle. Don't get stuck in the losses. They are inevitable. Instead, learn, adjust, grow, and move on to the next battle. You know there will always be another battle waiting for you.

I HAVE WALKED IN YOUR SHOES

I know the surprises that await you around almost every corner. Ours is not a relaxing business. I remember one particular surprise like it happened yesterday. In 2012, I interviewed for a position as a manager of talent acquisition at a medium-sized government contractor. The interview went exceptionally well, and within a couple of weeks, I was offered the position. My current employer was the manager of international recruiting and proposal recruiting at a very large government contractor. It was a tough decision to leave, but I felt a mid-sized firm would offer more opportunity and visibility. Though they weren't happy to see me go, I explained my professional objectives and they understood. In the end, everyone was excited for me, and wished me well.

My first day at my new job started normally. Erica, the director of talent acquisition, escorted me to my new office and showed me the essentials—copy machine, snack machine, bathrooms, the lunchroom, and various departments like finance and HR. It was pleasant and routine. I was settling in and drinking my first cup of coffee when Erica dropped a bombshell. She was pregnant and would be going on maternity leave in two months. I would be stepping into her role while she was away. Remember, I'd accepted a position as manager of talent acquisition, where I would be supporting their civil and personal technology division within the organization. Erica was now telling me I'd be asked to handle a more senior position with more responsibility across several divisions, and with much more visibility. I hadn't even been in my new job for eight hours or met the team yet. Needless to say, it was quite a first day.

I was anxious. Like every new employee, I needed to understand how the organization worked, its culture, its expectations, how job candidates perceived the company, how my recruiting team performed, and so forth. But now, I needed to learn these things quickly and consider how others might perceive the new kid on the block being promoted to a senior position—albeit temporarily—on his first day of work. I went home that night and talked to my family, friends, and a few trusted professional colleagues. By the next morning, I knew I'd have to face my fears and embrace this new opportunity.

On the second day of my new job, I met Bill, a former Navy captain who ran one of the organization's largest divisions. He was a very straightforward, no-nonsense kind of guy. Let's get it done type of leader, which I appreciated and respected. He and I built a very respectable relationship, um, during my time with the organization. And especially in the first couple of months, he understood how I liked the work I'm about results. He was about results. So naturally, we got along just fine. He was unaware that there would be a change in that Erica was going on maternity leave, uh, and a couple of months. But again, we grew to, uh, build a solid relationship and knew how each other worked. He understood my passions, drive, work ethic, and I understood his expectations. So he wasn't perturbed in any way, shape, or form, and embraced the fact that I would be taken on a larger role within the organization in such a short.

Two months passed extremely fast. It felt more like a week, but suddenly it was the Friday before Erica was expected to go on maternity leave for at least eight to ten weeks, possibly longer. She had prepared an announcement to be sent to the entire leadership team and all of the organization's employees. At that point, the company had about two thousand employees based in the Washington, DC metro area; Huntsville, Alabama; Texas; and California. The communication said I would be the acting director of talent acquisition, and all talent decisions would go through me. Remember, this was during the first two months of my tenure with the organization. I hadn't even gotten my footing yet, but there I was, thrown into a key role. I had to embrace the opportunity, and I had to give it my all.

WHEN THE BALL IS IN YOUR COURT

I was still experiencing some anxiety. I wondered how I would be perceived—especially with the torch being passed so quickly and to a brand new employee. I knew I was an extremely fortunate to get this type of exposure so early in my tenure. It would allow the organization to assess my leadership abilities almost immediately, which would likely open up more opportunities for me. Most people don't get career opportunities like this. I was grateful. Other managers who had been with the organization longer than me had not been asked to step into Erica's role. Instead, it was decided I was a better fit based on my previous success managing large groups and leading recruiting teams at a large organization. I shared the news with my family and friends. They all were excited for me and offered their best advice. But before I could fully process what was happening, Erica's last day at work arrived and it was time for me to step into my new position.

As I came into the office, I was greeted by my new staff. Bagels and coffee were set out to welcome me. I went to sit in Erica's office and assume my new position as acting director of talent acquisition. Within the first two hours in my new role, we received notice that we had won a very large contract for the civil and technical division. The project was slated to start in 45 to 60 days, so the hires needed to be made very quickly. The project was for a new client, so we couldn't just transfer over existing employees to support the new business. For this client, we would have to go out and recruit a new group of talent. They needed somewhere between 80 and 150 employees to work in downtown Washington, DC, and they needed them fast.

My first big test in my new position had arrived in record time—on my very first day on the job. I had to rally my team around delivering on a huge project that would bring in millions of dollars of revenue, and big exposure for our organization. I'd have to build trust with my team quickly. Fortunately, I had been in a similar situation before, not through my title, but more through the responsibilities I'd held as a manager of international recruiting. That position had been very fast paced with big deliverables and inflexible delivery dates, just like this new project. Luckily, this past experience had prepared me for the rigorous cadence of recruiting lots of people on a very tight deadline. I took a deep breath and prepared to rise to the occasion and successfully lead my new team through this exciting, but daunting challenge.

My previous experience came in handy. I knew that

all the hiring functions needed to work in concert to move swiftly and efficiently through the hiring process—otherwise, the whole thing would fall apart. Recruiting had to be closely tied into HR. HR had to be closely tied into operations. Operations had to be closely tied into facilities, and so forth - the entire process needed to be streamlined like an efficient assembly line. That's the only way we could move candidates through the hiring process fast enough to meet requirements in front of us. We could not afford any bottlenecks, or time gaps, or our hiring solution would collapse, and we would not be able to meet the client's needs.

There was a lot at stake, but we worked like a well-oiled machine. I communicated daily with the senior vice president of the division, where the work was being performed. I held daily meetings with human resources and my recruiting staff to keep the pulse on how well we were doing. Were we finding enough of the right candidates? Were the operations managers extending offers quickly with the help of human resources? Were the candidates accepting our offers? The answers were all yes. Everything was going extremely well, and we were able to get our first 20 hires within the first three weeks. This was quite a feat and gave us the momentum we needed to steam forward. In fact, we were able to staff up to 80 of the open positions within our first month and a half, which was more than enough. The expectation was only to get about 60 in the first couple of weeks, and then a streamlined approach or a staggered approach to have everyone onboarded by 45 or 60 days. We delivered what the client needed on time, and they were very pleased. Success!

Erica eventually returned to work after about ten weeks of maternity leave. I prepared a report for her to bring her up to speed on what had happened while she was out. Though I had not been in contact with Erica during her absence, unbeknownst to me, she had received feedback from members of the senior leadership team about my performance, professionalism, and how I had led the recruiting team while she was away. She read my report and called me into her office. Erica shared that she was very pleased and appreciative of the work I had done. We were both happy that there had been no major hiccups during her absence. I had not had to pull her back into the office to put at any fires. As a result, she had been able to fully enjoy her leave, rest after her child's birth, and be completely present for her newborn. For this, she was very grateful.

Erica became very instrumental in my career growth for the next four years. She championed my projects and communicated my ideas and concerns to the senior leadership team. She offered me many opportunities to lead different groups and projects. Eventually, our company was purchased by another organization, and Erica went on to pursue a different career in another state. We stayed in touch. She advised me through the transition after the acquisition. Her counsel was wise, and my decision to stay ultimately led to many professional opportunities.

STAY CALM WHEN THE BALL IS IN YOUR COURT

My point in sharing this story is important: Although I was thrust into an unexpected situation in a new position, I chose to overcome my fears and take advantage of the opportunity presented to me. I had to have faith in myself to make the right decision. You've got to have faith in yourself, too. It's the only way to grow in your career and to win the *Talent War!* Even though I was still new to the recruiting field, I was able to accomplish the goals placed on my plate and meet the professional expectations of my new company. The situation could have gone the other way. I could have failed—no one is always successful in their endeavors, right? It was a big risk. But even if I had failed, I still would have learned from the experience. In our industry, experience is one of the best teachers. That's why you've got to be willing to fall and skin your knees sometimes. But when the wins come—and they will, if you keep learning and growing as a recruiter—your confidence will grow. My confidence was off the charts after I successfully completed my unexpected assignment. I had faced my fears, done the hard work necessary to achieve my goals, and ultimately come out stronger. This experience gave me the courage to move forward in my career. I knew I could take on large projects and create effective recruiting strategies because I had already successfully done it.

Here's what I have learned about fear: sometimes, it can become a catalyst for personal and professional growth. Your anxiety can become your motivation. You can't let fear, anxiety, or inexperience rule your recruiting career—so flip it. Make overcoming these roadblocks your mission. Power through, be open to inevitable mistakes, grow, and learn. This mindset is the foundation of a successful career on the front lines of the *Talent War!* My professional story is proof that believing in yourself, owning what you know, and taking on new challenges and situations with confidence leads to success. Learning to trust myself was ultimately what lead to start my own company. I'll often reference the story in this chapter when I explain how I came to open my own consulting firm. I'm glad I didn't talk myself out of taking advantage of such a great opportunity.

CONCLUSION

Hopefully, after reading this book, you've been able to pick up on some of the challenges you'll face on the front lines of the *Talent War!* I also hope you'll find in these pages solid solutions to those challenges, new thinking, and strategies around hiring as well as common approaches to some of the most persistent problems that we all face when designing, implementing, and executing an effective hiring process. In sharing my professional challenges and opportunities over the last twenty-five-plus years, I hope I have been able to demonstrate with real-life stories how organizations of all sizes can take a deep dive into their current hiring process and figure out how to implement and execute more effective and efficient hiring strategies. Hopefully, I've also made it clear what's at stake if organizations don't confront their broken hiring process. As I've said many times throughout these pages, the stakes are high.

One common misconception about the hiring process is that once you have an effective one in place, you're good to go—you are finished. That's false because, at any given time, the hiring process can be disrupted by things that are totally out of your control. Unforeseen factors can throw even the most efficient hiring process off the rails. I encourage my clients and colleagues past and present to constantly] audit their current hiring process to ensure that all the controls are still running efficiently. If they're not, you have to be willing and able to identify, address, and change things to continue hiring effectively.

Most organizations feel that the best way to attack the problem and fix their broken hiring process is by adding more resources and people to the process. Unfortunately, that rarely gets to the heart of the problem. What leadership teams really should do is take a deep dive into their hiring process. Like a skilled surgeon, leaders in the hiring space need to diagnose why the patient is ill first, rather than bringing more surgeons into the operating room. Once they have an effective diagnosis, they can go in and address the problem with the right treatment. See what I mean? When you look at it this way, adding more people to a broken process doesn't make sense. Hiring more recruiting staff or more people to the interview process might be a comfortable thing to do, but it's not the right thing to do. It's actually dangerous to put a bandage on the problem. It certainly won't stop the bleeding, and you are likely to miss an opportunity to diagnose the real issues that are festering and threatening your company's health and bottom line.

There's no magic bullet when it comes to running an

effective hiring process. The only thing that will solve a broken hiring process is an effective diagnosis of the problems, creating targeted solutions to address those problems, and swift action to put solutions in place. I hope reading *Talent War!* has helped you think more creatively and holistically about how to fix your broken hiring process. My goals are to help you and your organization improve your hiring process. I hope the strategies and stories that I have shared will provide the guidance you need to make your hiring process more efficient and effective. I hope you'll share any nuggets of wisdom that you have gleaned from these pages with your team and colleagues. It will help you remember that you're not alone in the *Talent War!* And, if you need a hand, I'm always here to help.

Made in the USA
Columbia, SC
29 October 2020

23647648R00076